PENGUIN BOOKS

COMMON SENSE

THOMAS PAINE was born Thomas Pain in Thetford, England, on January 29, 1737, the son of a poor corset-maker. At age sixteen, Paine ran away from home and enlisted as a sailor on an English privateer, but he soon returned to his father's corset-making trade. In 1762, he began work as an excise collector, and in 1772, he wrote his first political pamphlet, *The Case of the Officers of Excise*, about the poor working conditions and wages for the officers of the excise. Shortly afterward he was fired from his job.

Paine came to America in 1774 with the encouragement of Benjamin Franklin, who provided Paine with a letter of recommendation. He was appointed editor of *The Pennsylvania Magazine* and became active in the call for American independence from England. His revolutionary pamphlet *Common Sense* was published in January of 1776, mobilizing public opinion in favor of independence from British rule. Soon after the successful revolution, Paine fell out of political favor. He spent the next fifteen years of his life in England and France (where he spent a year in prison during the French Revolution's Reign of Terror), and wrote several more political pamphlets, including *Rights of Man* (1790), *The Age of Reason* (1794), and *Agrarian Justice* (1796).

In 1802 Paine returned to the United States, where he died in June of 1809. He was buried on his small farm in New Rochelle, New York.

RICHARD BEEMAN, the John Welsh Centennial Professor of History Emeritus at the University of Pennsylvania, has previously served as the Chair of the Department of History, Associate Dean in Penn's School of Arts and Sciences, and Dean of the College of Arts and Sciences. He serves as a trustee of the National Constitution Center and on the center's executive committee. Author of seven previous books, among them *The Penguin Guide to the United States Constitution* and *Plain Honest Men: The Making of the American Constitution*, Professor Beeman has received numerous grants and awards, including fellowships from the National Endowment for the Humanities, the Rockefeller Foundation, the Institute for Advanced Study at Princeton, and the Huntington Library. His biography of Patrick Henry was a finalist for the National Book Award.

COMMON SENSE

THOMAS PAINE

EDITED WITH AN INTRODUCTION BY
RICHARD BEEMAN

SERIES EDITOR
RICHARD BEEMAN

PENGUIN BOOKS

PENGUIN BOOKS

Published by the Penguin Group

Penguin Group (USA) Inc., 375 Hudson Street, New York, New York 10014, U.S.A.
Penguin Group (Canada), 90 Eglinton Avenue East, Suite 700, Toronto, Ontario,
Canada M4P 2Y3 (a division of Pearson Penguin Canada Inc.)
Penguin Books Ltd, 80 Strand, London WC2R 0RL, England
Penguin Ireland, 25 St Stephen's Green, Dublin 2, Ireland
(a division of Penguin Books Ltd)
Penguin Group (Australia), 250 Camberwell Road, Camberwell, Victoria 3124,
Australia (a division of Pearson Australia Group Pty Ltd)
Penguin Books India Pvt Ltd, 11 Community Centre,
Panchsheel Park, New Delhi - 110 017, India
Penguin Group (NZ), 67 Apollo Drive, Rosedale, Auckland 0632, New Zealand (a
division of Pearson New Zealand Ltd)
Penguin Books (South Africa) (Pty) Ltd, 24 Sturdee Avenue, Rosebank,
Johannesburg 2196, South Africa

Penguin Books Ltd, Registered Offices:
80 Strand, London WC2R 0RL, England

First published in the United States of America by R. Bell 1776
This edition with a book introduction and a series introduction by Richard Beeman
published in Penguin Books 2012

1 3 5 7 9 10 8 6 4 2

Book introduction and series introduction copyright © Richard Beeman, 2012
All rights reserved

LIBRARY OF CONGRESS CATALOGING-IN-PUBLICATION DATA
Paine, Thomas, 1737–1809.
Common sense / Thomas Paine ; edited with an introduction
by Richard Beeman.
p.   cm.—(Penguin civic classics)
Includes bibliographical references.
ISBN 978-0-14-312200-5
1. United States—Politics and government—1775–1783.   2. Political science—
History—18th century.   3. Monarchy.   4. Political science—Early works to
1800.   I. Beeman, Richard R. II. Title.
E211.P1455 2012
973.3—dc23   2012020981

Printed in the United States of America
Set in Adobe Caslon
Designed by Sabrina Bowers

ALWAYS LEARNING   PEARSON

CONTENTS

COMMON SENSE

THE AMERICAN CRISIS I

We introduce the Penguin Civic Classics series by presenting our readers with a paradox. On the one hand, there is an abundance of evidence establishing that the vast majority of Americans, whatever their political differences, have an intense love of their country, believing that it has been one of the most successful experiments in human freedom and opportunity that the world has ever seen. And Americans are similarly united in having a deep reverence for their Constitution, for their institutions of government, and for the system of free enterprise that has been such a powerful engine for our economic growth. Americans see all of these as playing a vital role in making the nation as successful as it has been.

But there is an equally large body of evidence suggesting that Americans' knowledge of their history and of the way in which their institutions have worked over the course of that history is embarrassingly meager. For example, a third of Americans believe that the Declaration of Independence was written after the end of the Civil War, and fewer than half can identify the three branches of our federal government. Nearly 40 percent of the students at fifty-five of America's elite colleges and universities could not place the Civil War in the correct half century, and fewer than half of them, when presented with the text of the Gettysburg Address, were able to identify it. Nor does it appear that our knowledge improves much as we move closer to the present. Another survey has revealed that more than half of high school seniors thought that Italy, Germany, or Japan was a U.S. ally during the Second World War, and only 14 percent of those seniors could name any relevant fact about U.S. involvement in the Korean War. As the distinguished historian David McCullough has lamented, "While the clamorous popular culture races on, the American past is slipping away, out of sight and out of mind. We are losing our story, forgetting who we are and what it's taken to come this far."

With these discouraging results in front of us, it is no wonder that there is a growing clamor for an increased emphasis on "civic education," defined by one leading authority as "the cultivation of the virtues, knowledge, and skills" necessary for carrying out one's role as a citizen. That very phrase, "civic education," sounds to many like a doctor's prescription: "You need to take your medicine! It may not be very pleasant, but it is something you need to do in order to ensure not only your own health but also the health of the body politic." It is our hope that reading these volumes in the Penguin Civic Classics series will be much more pleasant than taking medicine, for although these volumes will indeed help improve the reader's civic *knowledge,* we also hope that they will provide some civic *inspiration*—a genuine appreciation for, even an excitement about, some of the words, ideas, and actions that have shaped American society and government since the nation's founding.

The history represented in these volumes, from the founding of the American colonies in the seventeenth century to the adoption of America's Declaration of Independence to Abraham Lincoln's inspiring Gettysburg Address to Barack Obama's inaugural address as the first African American president in American history, is not merely a collection of names and dates to be memorized but, rather, a set of stories to be absorbed and enjoyed. And they are stories that have a real relevance and meaning to our lives today, whether we are debating the nature of America's immigration laws, the extent to which the federal government should be involved in decisions relating to our health care, or, getting even closer to home, whether local schools and school districts have the constitutional right to search a student's locker.

In these volumes, the reader will encounter nearly all the central themes in American history, as well as the dilemmas and conflicts that have provided much of the dynamism and excitement of that history. The central themes and ideas of American public life—democracy, equality, economic opportunity, the role of government in maintaining that delicate balance between public order and personal freedom, and the government's responsibility to protect certain individual rights—have never remained static, nor have they ever elicited uniform agreement among American citizens.

The very first item in Terry Golway's collection of important American speeches is a sermon given by Massachusetts governor John Winthrop, aboard the ship *Arbella,* as it transported the first Puritan settlers to the new colony. In that sermon, Winthrop described the Puritans' mission in Massachusetts Bay as one of creating a "city upon a hill," a model of virtue and purity for all others in the world to follow. But his vision of that society was in some important respects very much at odds with the values that guide America today. In the opening words of his sermon, Winthrop reminded his fellow colonists that "GOD ALMIGHTY in His most holy and wise providence, hath so disposed of the condition of mankind, as in all times some must be rich, some poor, some high and eminent in power and dignity; others mean and in submission." Hardly a prescription for the democratic society that we claim to be today.

Fast-forward 136 years to the promise contained in Thomas Jefferson's Declaration of Independence that "all men are created equal"—a view of society *very* different from that articulated by Winthrop. Jefferson's city upon a hill was to be a nation dedicated to equality and the pursuit of happiness, not to a divinely ordained, inegalitarian social hierarchy. But, of course, in a world in which Africans were enslaved, women were considered legally subordinate to men, and, indeed, many free white males were denied the right to vote because they did not own the requisite amount of property, Jefferson's promise of equality fell far short of an accurate description of the reality of American society in 1776. Still, words have power, and Abraham Lincoln, for one, knew the power of those words. As is amply displayed in Allen Guelzo's volume containing many of Lincoln's principal speeches, time and time again Lincoln invoked Jefferson's preamble as a pledge that Americans of his age were honor-bound to fulfill, describing the preamble as "the electric cord in that Declaration that links the hearts of patriotic and liberty-loving men together, that will link those patriotic hearts as long as the love of freedom exists in the minds of men throughout the world."

Alas, Americans would fight a horrific, bloody

civil war in which more than 600,000 people, slave and free, lost their lives before the nation was able to take the steps necessary to forge the link to which Lincoln had referred. Beginning in December 1865, with the adoption of the Thirteenth Amendment, eliminating the institution of slavery; continuing with the adoption of the Fourteenth Amendment (July 1868), with its guarantee of "equal protection under the laws"; and culminating with the adoption of the Fifteenth Amendment (February 1870), asserting that the right to vote could not "be abridged . . . on account of race, color, or previous condition of servitude," those ideas of democracy and equality began to be incorporated into our constitutional system. But although those three amendments represented an important step forward, America's struggle to live up to the promise of the preamble was far from over. It took until 1920 for the nation to adopt the Nineteenth Amendment, giving women the right to vote, and in spite of the guarantees of the Fourteenth and Fifteenth Amendments, the civil rights of African Americans, including the right to vote, continued to be undermined by the actions of individual state governments well into the twentieth century. When Lyndon Johnson, only the second (after Woodrow Wilson) Southern-born president since the Civil War, signed into law the Voting Rights Act of 1965, he too quoted the preamble to the Declaration of Independence and ended his speech with a phrase from the anthem of the civil rights movement of the 1950s and 1960s: "We Shall Overcome." And when the first African American president, Barack Obama, delivered his inauguration speech on a cold day in January 2009, he began by paraphrasing the words of Thomas Jefferson's preamble, urging Americans "to carry forward that precious gift, that noble idea, passed on from generation to generation: the God-given promise that all are equal, all are free, and all deserve a chance to pursue their full measure of happiness." Even in 2009 those words were, like Jefferson's, expressions of hope, not descriptions of reality. But they have proved powerful indeed, and they continue to be a dynamic force in shaping the American future just as they have the American past

Another important theme that emerges from these volumes of Civic Classics involves the age-old debate on how and where to strike the best balance between public order and personal liberty. For most of human history, those who held government power—kings or emperors or czars—usually dealt with that issue by ruthlessly imposing their own definition of what was good for the masses of people whom they governed. When Thomas Paine published his earth-shaking pamphlet *Common Sense* in January 1776, his primary purpose was to persuade the American colonists to throw off British rule, but one of the key elements in his argument was the notion that while every society needs some form of government in order to provide security and protect the freedom of its citizens, the best and freest societies are those in which government is least intrusive. In Paine's words: "Society in every state is a blessing, but government even in its best state is but a necessary evil; in its worst state an intolerable one." Paine's words struck a chord with his American readers, who were already suspicious of the overly powerful, distant government of Great Britain, and the Declaration of Independence, approved seven months later, reinforced that same theme. The distrust of concentrations of government power—the notion that government, while necessary, must be restrained—is deeply rooted in America's revolutionary past and, of course, is very much alive today, as we can observe by the vitality of political movements such as the Tea Party.

As powerful as Paine's and Jefferson's indictments of excessive British power may have been, they did not provide the answer to the question of how the independent American nation could create a government that would strike an ideal balance between order and liberty. The men who gathered in Philadelphia in the summer of 1787 to frame a new constitution for their still-fragile independent nation took a giant step forward in providing an answer when they created a governmental system based on the division of power between the individual states and the central government—the system that we now call federalism—and by further dividing power among the three branches of the federal government in a system that we characterize as one of "checks and balances."

But, as in so many other important ideas in American history, those involving federalism and checks and balances were subject to many different interpretations. Alexander Hamilton, James Madison, and John Jay, in the eighty-five essays comprising *The Federalist Papers,* attempted to address some of the concerns that Americans had about the excessive power of the proposed new federal government and, in the process, provided Americans with enduring insights about government and politics—insights that are still cited by Supreme Court justices in their judicial opinions today. But Hamilton and Madison, the two principal authors of *The Federalist Papers,* began to disagree about the relationship of the new federal government to the individual states and to the people at large almost from the moment the government commenced operation. The debate over the way the words of the Constitution should be interpreted, with Madison and Jefferson taking a "strict construction" position, and Hamilton, George Washington, and others arguing for a broader interpretation of the Constitution, has stayed with us until the present day. As readers of Jay Feinman's collection of landmark Supreme Court cases will discover, the Court has spent a significant portion of its time over the years, beginning with Chief Justice John Marshall's majority opinion in *McCulloch v. Maryland* (1819), wrestling with the extent of and limits on federal government power. Nor has that conflict been confined to judicial or intellectual arguments. In the years leading up to the Civil War, Northern and Southern politicians fought ferocious battles over the question of what authority the federal government had to legislate with respect to the expansion of slavery into new territories; once again, the ever-eloquent Abraham Lincoln weighed in on those issues, as is amply illustrated in Allen Guelzo's selection of Lincoln speeches. In the end, of course, it was not words that settled the constitutional argument between North and South but the force of arms. The Civil War was, in some senses, America's greatest civic failure, for knowledge and reason alone were not sufficient to settle the conflict between North and South. But however terrible the toll, it did resolve the paradox at the nation's core—the existence of the institution of slavery in a nation that claimed to be devoted to liberty.

Mercifully, the Civil War was the last occasion in which our differences of opinion over governmental power have resulted in warfare, but the war of words has never ceased. Whether debating issues relating to economic regulation or immigration, or providing and regulating health care, Americans—Republicans and Democrats, Tea

Party members and Occupy Wall Street activists—
continue to differ, sometimes passionately, on the
way our Constitution should be interpreted.

Americans, perhaps more than any other people
in the world, have been ardently committed to defending their "rights." Indeed, when most Americans today think of their Constitution, they think
not so much about those enumerated powers such
as the levying of taxes, the regulating of commerce,
or the coining of money that are contained in the
main body of the Constitution, but, rather, they
think of the Bill of Rights. In fact, one of the few
mistakes made by the framers of the Constitution
in 1787 was their failure even to include a Bill of
Rights in their final draft of the Constitution, a
mistake that was, fortunately, remedied by the First
Federal Congress in 1789. The rights articulated in
our first ten amendments, including freedom of
speech, the "free exercise of religion," freedom of the
press, and freedom from unlawful search and seizure, have not only provided the foundation for the
freedoms that we so value today but have also
prompted some of our most vigorously debated
controversies. Readers of Jay Feinman's volume on
some of the most important Supreme Court decisions in our history will discover that, in general, the
Court's definition of the rights guaranteed in those
amendments has tended to widen over the course
of our history. But there remain limits on the Bill
of Rights protections enjoyed by Americans. For

example, the right of free speech has not extended to public protests in which the threat of violence is imminent, and in an era of GPS tracking devices and CCTV cameras, Americans are confronted with new challenges in defining what constitutes an unlawful search and seizure.

The constitutional protection of individual rights has not been confined to those items specifically listed in the Bill of Rights. The Ninth Amendment, which says that the "enumeration in the Constitution, of certain rights, shall not be construed to deny or disparage others retained by the people," has been interpreted to include the right of privacy, including the right of a woman to have some control over her health and reproductive decisions. The most well known of the Supreme Court decisions relating to the right of a woman to terminate a pregnancy, *Roe v. Wade* (1973), far from settling that difficult question, has been followed by a series of subsequent Supreme Court decisions seeking to further refine and, in many cases, limit the right to obtain an abortion. The Court's decisions in these areas, far from being legal abstractions of interest only to a few history or civics teachers, have had an impact, and will continue to have an impact, on the lives of millions of women.

This series of Penguin Civic Classics is based on the belief that acquiring knowledge of America's history and of our rights and responsibilities as citizens is not merely an abstract, academic exercise. *It really matters.* It can make an actual difference in each and every one of our lives. And never more so than in the extraordinarily complicated, tumultuous, twenty-first-century world in which we live—a time of rapid, sometimes confounding, change. David McCullough has spoken of the way in which our knowledge of history and of the way in which our institutions of government operate can give us a "sense of navigation, a sense of what we've been through in times past and who we are." It can also *empower* us. If we are familiar with the way in which people in the past have confronted their problems, and if we have a decent understanding of how to make the best use of America's institutions to deal with the problems confronting us in the present, we have a much better chance of being able to control our own destinies. Our opinions of the "correct" way to proceed may not always prevail, but we will at least be participants, not passive bystanders, in the ongoing drama that is the history of the United States. And, perhaps most important of all, it is often personally more rewarding, more fun, to be a participant rather than to be a bystander.

RICHARD BEEMAN

INTRODUCTION

Thomas Paine's *Common Sense* may well be the most influential piece of polemical writing in all of American history. It helped change the course of history in the western world, giving to Americans the intellectual rationale *and* the self-confidence to cast off the rule of what at that time was the most powerful nation on earth, Great Britain. And it gave Americans a vision of an independent future that marked a revolutionary break with past conceptions of government, of constitutions, and of the very nature of society itself. Perhaps most remarkably, it was written by an impoverished, mostly self-educated English immigrant who had arrived in America just a little more than a year before its publication. A very *angry* Englishman, who had encountered little other than failure and rejection before his arrival on American shores.

A LIFE OF FRUSTRATION IN ENGLAND

Thomas Pain (he did not add the "e" to his last name until the second edition of *Common Sense* appeared) was born in the small English village of Thetford, in the eastern lowland county of Norfolk, on January 29, 1737. His Quaker father, Joseph Pain, earned his living as a staymaker—a maker of corsets, those contraptions composed of leather or linen which, with their ribs of steel or whalebone and laced together on the sides with ribbon, enabled (or constrained) the women of eighteenth-century England to present themselves as narrow-waisted and amply-bosomed. Pain's Anglican mother, Frances, was the daughter of one of Thetford's most successful lawyers. An odd pairing it was—in those days Quakers were viewed as highly-suspect dissenters from the established Anglican religion and Joseph Pain's profession placed him solidly in the lower class, whereas Frances came from a family comfortably situated in England's upper middle class.

The marriage of Joseph and Frances was a formula for *downward*, not upward mobility, and the only way the family was able to afford to send young Tom to grammar school from the ages of six to thirteen was by borrowing money from Joseph's sister-in-law. At the age of thirteen Tom left school to begin his apprenticeship in what was so often the fate of the son of a poor man—dragged in his father's footsteps to learn the craft of staymaking. Although he would end up spending more than a dozen years in the trade, he hated it; at the age of sixteen he ran away from home and enlisted to serve as a buccaneer aboard the English privateer *Terrible*, under the command of one William Death. Pain's father scurried to London and was able to talk his son out of his career change—and a good thing too, for at the very beginning of its voyage the *Terrible* fell prey to a French privateer, losing more than 150 of its 175-man crew, including the appropriately named Captain Death.

Pain had escaped death, but that escape meant a return to the staymaking trade he so loathed. A few years later he deserted his trade again, serving for a while on another English privateer, but by 1758 he went back to staymaking in the southeastern seaside town of Dover. A year later, Pain set up his own staymaking shop in nearby Sandwich, and a year after that he met and married Mary Lambert, a maid to a local shopkeeper's wife—a marriage that ended tragically with her death the following year. In 1762 he changed professions, passing the qualifying exam to become an excise collector. He was suspended from his post three years later for having claimed to have inspected goods that he had not really inspected. So it was back to staymaking, and then, for a few years, to a position as a part-time teacher at an academy in London. In 1768 he was re-admitted to the customs service in the town of Lewes, and in 1771 married Elizabeth Ollive, the daughter of a tobacconist in whose house he was lodging. The marriage was a disaster, with the two parting, never bothering to obtain a divorce, without the union ever being consummated.

About that time Pain began to hang out in the taverns and coffeehouses of Lewes, where he indulged not only his fondness for drink, but also his fondness for *words*. It was his ability as a wordsmith that caused Pain's fellow excisemen to persuade him to draft a petition to Parliament asking for an increase in their salaries. *The Case of the Officers of Excise,* Pain's first polemical effort, gives us our first hint of what was to come. Its structure was logical, its style plainspoken, and its tone passionate and angry. After completing his petition, Pain traveled to London, where he spent the better part of a year, without leave from the excise service, attempting to lobby members of Parliament to pay heed to the plight of the excisemen. Pain's petition was not only ignored, but considered incendiary and subversive, and on April 8, 1774, the Board of Excise fired him, suggesting that he might be liable to arrest on account of his failure to collect the required excises that had accumulated during his absence. No wife, no job, facing the threat of imprisonment—Thomas Pain was by this time nurturing a deep-seated anger about the unfairness of life in the kingdom ruled by King George III.

Shortly after these disasters had befallen him, Pain paid a visit to 36 Craven Street, the London residence of the renowned experimental scientist and influential American colonial agent, Benjamin Franklin. When Pain took his leave of Franklin that day, he carried with him a letter addressed to Franklin's son-in-law, Richard Bache, but intended as a general introduction to the community of merchants and artisans of Philadelphia:

> The bearer Mr. Thomas Pain is very well recommended to me as an ingenious, worthy young man. He goes to Pennsylvania with a view of settling there. If you can put him in a way of obtaining employment as a clerk, or assistant tutor in a school, or assistant surveyor, of all of which I think him very capable, so that he may procure a subsistence at least, till he can make acquaintance and obtain a knowledge of the country, you will do well, and much oblige your affectionate father.

A NEW BEGINNING

Using a small sum of money that he had obtained from his estranged wife's family in return for his promise not to make any claim to ownership of their house and possessions, Pain embarked on his voyage to America aboard the ship *London Packet* in October 1774. It was a horrific voyage.

He spent most of his time below decks suffering from a combination of seasickness and what may have been typhus, finally reaching Philadelphia on November 30, 1774, where he was carried off the ship on a stretcher. He spent the next six weeks recovering in a boardinghouse on Philadelphia's waterfront and then, after regaining his strength, presented his letter of introduction to Benjamin Franklin's son-in-law.

In early January of 1775, Pain fell into conversation with Robert Aitken, a printer and entrepreneur who was starting a new project, *The Pennsylvania Magazine; or American Monthly Museum.* Aitken hired Pain as editor of his new magazine, where he set about writing a series of essays. The essays ranged widely, from lighthearted pieces on marriage to pieces on serious topics such as the iniquity of the institution of slavery and the subordinate status of women.

Although Pain had begun to find his voice when he wrote *The Case of the Officers of the Excise,* as a writer for the *Pennsylvania Magazine* he had found a platform from which to broadcast his voice. But sometime in the fall of 1775, Pain's cantankerous nature put him in conflict with his employer, and by late October of that year Pain and Aitken had parted ways. It would be a decision with momentous consequences. Now unencumbered by his editorial responsibilities, Pain began work on an essay on the steadily escalating conflict between the American colonies and Great Britain.

THE REVOLUTIONARY CHARACTER OF *COMMON SENSE*

By the time that Pain sat down to write *Common Sense,* the American colonies and Great Britain were at war, but the constitutional conflict between the two adversaries dated back to at least 1763, the year in which the king and Parliament began to reorganize their empire in the aftermath of England's victory over the French and Spanish in the Seven Years War. It had been an expensive victory—the cost of the war had plunged the British treasury into debt, and the costs of protecting the territory acquired in the war would add to the debt. Beginning in 1764, the British Parliament began levying taxes on the colonies aimed at raising revenue to offset some of those increased costs. The British ministry also announced its intention of tightening up on the lax enforcement of customs laws that had marked the previous policy of "salutary neglect." In fact, the taxes imposed upon the colonies—a tax on imported molasses and a stamp tax, similar to taxes already in force in England—did not present a major economic burden to Americans. But the means by which the taxes were imposed—enacted by a distant Parliament without the colonists' consent—seemed to Americans to violate a fundamental principle of the English Constitution—that of "no taxation without representation."

American protests began with humble petitions from colonial assemblies, asking for a repeal of what they believed to be unconstitutional acts. But protests were not confined to humble petitions. Increasingly, ordinary folks in America's cities and towns joined the protest, taking to the streets with marches, demonstrations, and economic boycotts, which sometimes erupted into violence. American resistance bred reaction, and the British responded by sending troops to keep order in their colonies. The turning point came on the cold, moonlit night of December 16, 1773, when three groups of fifty Boston residents, disguised as Mohawk Indians, boarded three ships of the English East India Company and, in protest against a parliamentary act giving to the English trading company a monopoly on the sale of tea in America, dumped some ninety-two thousand pounds of tea into Boston harbor.

The British responded with a series of measures—the Coercive Acts—aimed not only at punishing the town of Boston, but also at suspending institutions of civil government in Massachusetts, thus significantly expanding the scope of the political and constitutional conflict. In response a "Continental Congress," composed of representatives of all the American colonies, began to meet in Philadelphia in September 1774. Members of the Congress were united in their determination to resist British policies such as the Coercive Acts, but divided over how to do so. Even after the outbreak of military conflict at Lexington and Concord in April 1775, the delegates to the Congress continued to argue over how to persuade the king and Parliament to return to what they called the "true principles of the English Constitution." Between April 1775 and January 1776, as the political and military conflict continued to escalate, many colonists began to consider independence as an option. But many others—particularly those from New York and Pennsylvania—continued to hope for reconciliation, basing their hopes on the belief that the British king would eventually come to his senses and abide by the true principles of their beloved English Constitution.

The publication of *Common Sense* would wholly change the debate over America's relationship with England and with England's vaunted "constitution." "The so much boasted constitution of England," Pain wrote, may have been "noble for the dark and slavish times in which it was erected. . . . But that it is imperfect, subject to convulsions, and incapable of producing what it seems to promise, is easily demonstrated." With that contemptuous dismissal, he embarked on a passionate attack on the very institutions that lay at the heart of the English Constitution. He reserved his greatest ire for the institution to which most Americans, even in January 1776, still felt their greatest loyalty—the English monarchy. "There is something exceedingly ridiculous," he observed, "in the composition of the monarchy; it first excludes a man from the means of information, yet empowers him in cases where the highest judgment is required." He continued his assault on the monarchy with a discourse on equality. "Mankind being originally equal in order of creation," he wrote, "the equality could only be destroyed by subsequent circumstances." Acknowledging with some regret the inequality that existed between rich and poor, Pain went on to condemn "another, even greater distinction, for which no truly natural or religious reason can be assigned, and that is the distinction of men into KINGS and SUBJECTS."

Pain then embarked on a survey of the history of monarchy, ridiculing it as "the most prosperous invention the Devil ever set on foot for the promotion of idolatry." Following his wrathful survey of the sins and "savage manners" of kings throughout the ages, he ended with his assessment of the English monarchy:

> England, since the conquest, hath known some few good monarchs, but groaned beneath a much larger number of bad ones; yet no man in his senses can say that their claim under William the

Conqueror is a very honorable one. A French bastard landing with an armed banditti, and establishing himself king of England against the consent of the natives, is in plain terms a very paltry rascally original. It certainly hath no divinity in it.

And King George III, "the royal brute of England," was among the worst of the lot. "Even brutes," Pain wrote, "do not devour their young, nor savages make war on their own families."

Pain's assault on the king is the most emotionally powerful part of his pamphlet, but there were two other important components in his argument in favor of independence. One of these—the "common sense" aspect of the pamphlet—sought to demonstrate the folly of an empire in which the colonies were required to occupy a subordinate position in relation to their "Mother Country." While America may have "flourished under the former connexion with Great Britain," it did not logically follow "that because a child has thrived on milk, that it is never to have meat, or that the first twenty years of our lives is to become a precedent for the next twenty." "Small islands not capable of protecting themselves, are the proper objects for kingdoms to take under their care," he concluded, "but there is something very absurd in supposing a continent to be perpetually governed by an island."

In what is perhaps the most stirring passage in

Common Sense, Pain looks to the future, to the opportunity that Americans had to form "the noblest, purest constitution on the face of the earth." "We have it in our power," he exulted, "to begin the world over again. . . . The birth-day of a new world is at hand, and a race of men perhaps as numerous as all Europe contains, are to receive their portion of freedom from the event of a few months."

America, indeed, the world, had never seen anything like *Common Sense*. The pamphlet sold more than 100,000 copies within three months of its publication, and perhaps as many as 250,000 within the first six months. And its impact went beyond its sales; as one Philadelphia writer observed, "it was read to all ranks"—farmers, artisans, mechanics, merchant seamen—in coffeehouses and taverns throughout America. It caused a fundamental transformation in Americans' thinking about both their relationship with their "Mother Country" and their very identity as Americans. As one Connecticut reader observed, "You have declared the sentiments of millions. Your production may justly be compared to a land flood that sweeps before it. We were blind, but on reading these enlightening words, the scales have fallen from our eyes."

The first printing of *Common Sense* identified its author as an "Englishman," but by the time of the second printing just a few weeks later, Thomas

Pain had added that "e" to the end of his name, and was not only owning up to his authorship of the pamphlet, but also proudly proclaiming his identity as an "American." And, truly, that was the revolutionary character of *Common Sense*. Before Tom Paine wrote *Common Sense*, most Americans were earnestly defending their liberties as *Englishmen*, but after its publication, more and more of the subjects of King George III were beginning to imagine an entirely different future as independent *Americans*.

RICHARD BEEMAN

SUGGESTIONS FOR FURTHER READING

The most recent, and authoritative, edition of the complete works of Thomas Paine is Eric Foner, ed., *Thomas Paine: Collected Writings* (New York: Library of America, 1995). The most detailed biographies of Paine are David Freeman Hawke, *Paine* (New York: Harper and Row, 1974) and Craig Nelson, *Thomas Paine: Enlightenment, Revolution, and the Birth of the Modern Nation* (New York: Penguin, 2007). For an excellent study of Paine and the coming of the American Revolution, see Eric Foner, *Tom Paine and Revolutionary America* (New York: Oxford University Press, 1976). Jack Fruchtman, *The Political Philosophy of Thomas Paine* (Baltimore: Johns Hopkins University Press, 2011) is an excellent study of the intellectual foundations of Paine's political writings.

A NOTE
ON THE TEXT

The text of *Common Sense* used here is Paine's second edition, published on 14 February 1776 by William and Thomas Bradford of Philadelphia, Pennsylvania. Paine published a significantly shorter first edition on 10 January 1776 with the Philadelphia firm of Robert Bell, then added the appendix and reply to the Quaker meeting of 20 January, both of which appear here, for his longer edition with new publishers.

COMMON SENSE

INTRODUCTION

Perhaps the sentiments contained in the following pages, are not yet sufficiently fashionable to procure them general favor; a long habit of not thinking a thing *wrong*, gives it a superficial appearance of being *right*, and raises at first a formidable outcry in defence of custom. But the tumult soon subsides. Time makes more converts than reason.

As a long and violent abuse of power, is generally the Means of calling the right of it in question (and in matters too which might never have been thought of, had not the Sufferers been aggravated into the inquiry) and as the K— of England had undertaken in his *own Right*, to support the Parliament in what he calls *Theirs*, and as the good people of this country are grievously oppressed by the combination, they have an undoubted privilege to inquire into the pretensions of both, and equally to reject the usurpation of either.

In the following sheets, the author hath studiously avoided every thing which is personal among ourselves. Compliments as well as censure to individuals make no part thereof. The wise, and the worthy, need not the triumph of a pamphlet; and those whose sentiments are injudicious, or unfriendly, will cease of themselves unless too much pains are bestowed upon their conversion.

The cause of America is in a great measure the cause of all mankind. Many circumstances hath, and will arise, which are not local, but universal, and through which the principles of all Lovers of Mankind are affected, and in the Event of which, their Affections are interested. The laying a Country desolate with Fire and Sword, declaring War against the natural rights of all Mankind, and extirpating the Defenders thereof from the Face of the Earth, is the Concern of every Man to whom Nature hath given the Power of feeling; of which Class, regardless of Party Censure, is the

AUTHOR.

P.S. The Publication of this new Edition hath been delayed, with a View of taking notice (had it been necessary) of any Attempt to refute the Doctrine of Independance: As no Answer hath yet appeared, it is now presumed that none will, the Time needful for getting such a Performance ready for the Public being considerably past.

Who the Author of this Production is, is wholly

unnecessary to the Public, as the Object for Attention is the *Doctrine itself*, not the *Man*. Yet it may not be unnecessary to say, That he is unconnected with any Party, and under no sort of Influence public or private, but the influence of reason and principle.

Philadelphia, February 14, 1776.

OF THE ORIGIN AND DESIGN OF GOVERNMENT IN GENERAL. WITH CONCISE REMARKS ON THE ENGLISH CONSTITUTION.

Some writers have so confounded society with government, as to leave little or no distinction between them; whereas they are not only different, but have different origins. Society is produced by our wants, and government by our wickedness; the former promotes our happiness *positively* by uniting our affections, the latter *negatively* by restraining our vices. The one encourages intercourse, the other creates distinctions. The first is a patron, the last a punisher.

Society in every state is a blessing, but government even in its best state is but a necessary evil; in its worst state an intolerable one; for when we suffer, or are exposed to the same miseries *by a government*, which we might expect in a country *without government*, our calamities is heightened by reflecting that we furnish the means by which we suffer. Government, like dress, is the badge of lost innocence; the palaces of kings are built on the ruins of the bowers of paradise. For were the impulses of conscience clear, uniform, and irresistibly obeyed, man would need no other lawgiver; but that not being the case, he finds it necessary to surrender up a part of his property to furnish means for the protection of the rest; and this he is induced to do by the same prudence which in every other case advises him out of two evils to choose the least. *Wherefore*, security being the true design and end of government, it unanswerably follows that whatever *form* thereof appears most likely to ensure it to us, with the least expence and greatest benefit, is preferable to all others.

In order to gain a clear and just idea of the design and end of government, let us suppose a small number of persons settled in some sequestered part of the earth, unconnected with the rest, they will then represent the first peopling of any country, or of the world. In this state of natural liberty, society will be their first thought. A thousand motives will excite them thereto, the strength of one man is so unequal to his wants, and his mind so unfitted for perpetual solitude, that he is soon obliged to seek assistance and relief of another, who in his turn requires the same. Four or five united would be able to raise a tolerable dwelling in the midst of a wilderness, but *one* man might labour out the common period of life without accomplishing any thing; when he had felled his timber he could not remove it, nor erect it after it was removed; hunger in the mean time would urge him from his work, and every different want call him a different way. Disease, nay even misfortune would be death, for though neither might be mortal, yet either would disable him from living, and reduce him to a state in which he might rather be said to perish than to die.

Thus necessity, like a gravitating power, would soon form our newly arrived emigrants into society, the reciprocal blessings of which, would supercede, and render the obligations of law and government unnecessary while they remained perfectly just to each other; but as nothing but heaven is impregnable to vice, it will unavoidably happen, that in proportion as they surmount the first difficulties of emigration, which bound them together in a common cause, they will begin to relax in their duty and attachment to each other; and this remissness, will point out the necessity, of establishing some form of government to supply the defect of moral virtue.

Some convenient tree will afford them a State-House, under the branches of which, the whole colony may assemble to deliberate on public matters. It is more than probable that their first laws will have the title only of REGULATIONS, and be enforced by no other penalty than public disesteem. In this first parliament every man, by natural right will have a seat.

But as the colony increases, the public concerns will increase likewise, and the distance at which the members may be separated, will render it too inconvenient for all of them to meet on every occasion as at first, when their number was small, their habitations near, and the public concerns few and trifling. This will point out the convenience of their consenting to leave the legislative part to be managed by a select number chosen from the whole body, who are supposed to have the same concerns at stake which those have who appointed them, and who will act in the same manner as the whole body would act were they present. If the colony continue increasing, it will become necessary to augment the number of the representatives, and that the interest of every part of the colony may be attended to, it will be found best to divide the whole into convenient parts, each part sending its proper number; and that the *elected* might never form to themselves an interest separate from the *electors*, prudence will point out the propriety of having elections often; because as the *elected* might by that means return and mix again with the general body of the *electors* in a few months, their fidelity to the public will be secured by the prudent reflexion of not making a rod for themselves. And as this frequent interchange will establish a common interest with every part of the community, they will mutually and naturally support each other, and on this (not on the unmeaning name of king) depends the *strength of government, and the happiness of the governed.*

Here then is the origin and rise of government; namely, a mode rendered necessary by the inability of moral virtue to govern the world; here too is the design and end of government, viz. freedom and security. And however our eyes may be dazzled with snow, or our ears deceived by sound; however prejudice may warp our wills, or interest darken our understanding, the simple voice of nature and of reason will say, it is right.

I draw my idea of the form of government from a principle in nature, which no art can overturn, viz. that the more simple any thing is, the less liable it is to be disordered, and the easier repaired when disordered; and with this maxim in view, I offer a few remarks on the so much boasted constitution of England. That it was noble for the dark and slavish times in which it was erected is granted. When the world was over-run with tyranny the least remove therefrom was a glorious rescue. But that it is imperfect, subject to convulsions, and incapable of producing what it seems to promise, is easily demonstrated.

Absolute governments (tho' the disgrace of human nature) have this advantage with them, that they are simple; if the people suffer, they know the head from which their suffering springs, know likewise the remedy, and are not bewildered by a variety of causes and cures. But the constitution of

England is so exceedingly complex, that the nation may suffer for years together without being able to discover in which part the fault lies, some will say in one and some in another, and every political physician will advise a different medicine.

I know it is difficult to get over local or long standing prejudices, yet if we will suffer ourselves to examine the component parts of the English constitution, we shall find them to be the base remains of two ancient tyrannies, compounded with some new republican materials.

First. – The remains of monarchical tyranny in the person of the king.

Secondly. – The remains of aristocratical tyranny in the persons of the peers.

Thirdly. – The new republican materials, in the persons of the commons, on whose virtue depends the freedom of England.

The two first, by being hereditary, are independent of the people; wherefore in a *constitutional sense* they contribute nothing towards the freedom of the state.

To say that the constitution of England is a *union* of three powers reciprocally *checking* each other, is farcical, either the words have no meaning, or they are flat contradictions.

To say that the commons is a check upon the king, presupposes two things.

First. – That the king is not to be trusted without being looked after, or in other words, that a thirst for absolute power is the natural disease of monarchy.

Secondly. – That the commons, by being appointed for that purpose, are either wiser or more worthy of confidence than the crown.

But as the same constitution which gives the commons a power to check the king by withholding the supplies, gives afterwards the king a power to check the commons, by empowering him to reject their other bills; it again supposes that the king is wiser than those whom it has already supposed to be wiser than him. A mere absurdity!

There is something exceedingly ridiculous in the composition of monarchy; it first excludes a man from the means of information, yet empowers him to act in cases where the highest judgment is required. The state of a king shuts him from the world, yet the business of a king requires him to know it thoroughly; wherefore the different parts, unnaturally opposing and destroying each other, prove the whole character to be absurd and useless.

Some writers have explained the English constitution thus; the king, say they, is one, the people another; the peers are an house in behalf of the king; the commons in behalf of the people; but this hath all the distinctions of an house divided against itself; and though the expressions be pleasantly arranged, yet when examined they appear idle and ambiguous; and it will always happen, that the nicest construction that words are capable of, when applied to the description of some thing which either cannot exist, or is too incomprehensible to be within the compass of description, will be words of sound only, and though they may amuse the ear, they cannot inform the mind, for this explanation includes a previous question, viz. *How came the king by a power which the people are afraid to trust, and always obliged to check?* Such a power could not be the gift of a wise people, neither can any power, *which needs checking*, be from God; yet the provision, which the constitution makes, supposes such a power to exist.

But the provision is unequal to the task; the means either cannot or will not accomplish the end, and the whole affair is a *felo de se*; for as the greater weight will always carry up the less, and as all the wheels of a machine are put in motion by one, it only remains to know which power in the constitution has the most weight, for that will govern; and though the others, or a part of them, may clog, or, as the phrase is, check the rapidity of its motion, yet so long as they cannot stop it, their endeavours will be ineffectual; the first moving power will at last have its way, and what it wants in speed is supplied by time.

That the crown is this overbearing part in the English constitution needs not be mentioned, and that it derives its whole consequence merely from being the giver of places and pensions is self-evident, wherefore, though we have been wise enough to shut and lock a door against absolute monarchy, we at the same time have been foolish enough to put the crown in possession of the key.

The prejudice of Englishmen, in favour of their own government by king, lords, and commons, arises as much or more from national pride than reason. Individuals are undoubtedly safer in England than in some other countries, but the *will* of the king is as much the *law* of the land in Britain as in France, with this difference, that instead of proceeding directly from his mouth, it is handed to the people under the most formidable shape of an act of parliament. For the fate of Charles the First, hath only made kings more subtle – not more just.

Wherefore, laying aside all national pride and prejudice in favour of modes and forms, the plain truth is, that *it is wholly owing to the constitution of the people, and not to the constitution of the government* that the crown is not as oppressive in England as in Turkey.

An inquiry into the *constitutional errors* in the English form of government is at this time highly necessary; for as we are never in a proper condition of doing justice to others, while we continue under the influence of some leading partiality, so neither are we capable of doing it to ourselves while we remain fettered by any obstinate prejudice. And as a man, who is attached to a prostitute, is unfitted to choose or judge of a wife, so any prepossession in favour of a rotten constitution of government will disable us from discerning a good one.

Mankind being originally equals in the order of creation, the equality could only be destroyed by some subsequent circumstance; the distinctions of rich, and poor, may in a great measure be accounted for, and that without having recourse to the harsh, ill-sounding names of oppression and avarice. Oppression is often the *consequence*, but seldom or never the *means* of riches; and though avarice will preserve a man from being necessitously poor, it generally makes him too timorous to be wealthy.

But there is another and greater distinction for which no truly natural or religious reason can be assigned, and that is, the distinction of men into Kings and Subjects. Male and female are the distinctions of nature, good and bad the distinctions of heaven; but how a race of men came into the world so exalted above the rest, and distinguished

...ke some new species, is worth enquiring into, and whether they are the means of happiness or of misery to mankind.

In the early ages of the world, according to the scripture chronology, there were no kings; the consequence of which was there were no wars; it is the pride of kings which throw mankind into confusion. Holland without a king hath enjoyed more peace for this last century than any of the monarchial governments in Europe. Antiquity favors the same remark; for the quiet and rural lives of the first patriarchs hath a happy something in them, which vanishes away when we come to the history of Jewish royalty.

Government by kings was first introduced into the world by the Heathens, from whom the children of Israel copied the custom. It was the most prosperous invention the Devil ever set on foot for the promotion of idolatry. The Heathens paid divine honors to their deceased kings, and the christian world hath improved on the plan by doing the same to their living ones. How impious is the title of *sacred majesty* applied to a worm, who in the midst of his splendor is crumbling into dust.

As the exalting one man so greatly above the rest cannot be justified on the equal rights of nature, so neither can it be defended on the authority of scripture; for the will of the Almighty, as declared by Gideon and the prophet Samuel, expressly disapproves of government by kings. All anti-monarchial parts of scripture have been very smoothly glossed over in monarchial governments, but they undoubtedly merit the attention of countries which have their governments yet to form. *'Render unto Cæsar the things which are Cæsar's'* is the scriptural doctrine of courts, yet it is no support of monarchial government, for the Jews at that time were without a king, and in a state of vassalage to the Romans.

Near three thousand years passed away from the Mosaic account of the creation, till the Jews under a national delusion requested a king. Till then their form of government (except in extraordinary cases, where the Almighty interposed) was a kind of republic administred by a judge and the elders of the tribes. Kings they had none, and it was held sinful to acknowledge any being under that title but the Lords of Hosts. And when a man seriously reflects on the idolatrous homage which is paid to the persons of Kings, he need not wonder, that the Almighty, ever jealous of his honor, should disapprove of a form of government which so impiously invades the prerogative of heaven.

Monarchy is ranked in scripture as one of the sins of the Jews, for which a curse in reserve is denounced against them. The history of that transaction is worth attending to.

The children of Israel being oppressed by the Midianites, Gideon marched against them with a small army, and victory, thro' the divine interposition, decided in his favour. The Jews elate with success, and attributing it to the generalship of Gideon, proposed making him a king, saying, *Rule thou over us, thou and thy son and thy son's son.* Here was temptation in its fullest extent; not a kingdom only, but an hereditary one, but Gideon in the piety of his soul replied, *I will not rule over you, neither shall my son rule over you,* THE LORD SHALL RULE OVER YOU. Words need not be more explicit; Gideon doth not *decline* the honor but denieth their right to give it; neither doth he compliment them with invented declarations of his thanks, but in the positive stile of a prophet charges them with disaffection to their proper sovereign, the King of Heaven.

About one hundred and thirty years after this, they fell again into the same error. The hankering which the Jews had for the idolatrous customs of the Heathens, is something exceedingly unaccountable; but so it was, that laying hold of the misconduct of Samuel's two sons, who were entrusted with some secular concerns, they came in an abrupt and clamourous manner to Samuel, saying, *Behold thou art old, and thy sons walk not in thy ways, now make us a king to judge us like all the other nations.* And here we cannot but observe that their motives were bad, viz. that they might be *like* unto other nations, i. e. the Heathens, whereas their true glory laid in being as much *unlike* them as possible. *But the thing displeased Samuel when they said, give us a king to judge us; and Samuel prayed unto the*

Lord, and the Lord said unto Samuel, Hearken unto the voice of the people in all that they say unto thee, for they have not rejected thee, but they have rejected me, THAT I SHOULD NOT REIGN OVER THEM. *According to all the works which they have done since the day that I brought them up out of Egypt, even unto this day; wherewith they have forsaken me and served other Gods; so do they also unto thee. Now therefore hearken unto their voice, howbeit, protest solemnly unto them and shew them the manner of the king that shall reign over them, i. e.* not of any particular king, but the general manner of the kings of the earth, whom Israel was so eagerly copying after. And notwithstanding the great distance of time and difference of manners, the character is still in fashion, *And Samuel told all the words of the Lord unto the people, that asked of him a king. And he said, This shall be the manner of the king that shall reign over you; he will take your sons and appoint them for himself for his chariots, and to be his horsemen, and some shall run before his chariots* (this description agrees with the present mode of impressing men) *and he will appoint him captains over thousands and captains over fifties, and will set them to ear his ground and to reap his harvest, and to make his instruments of war, and instruments of his chariots; and he will take your daughters to be confectionaries and to be cooks and to be bakers* (this describes the expence and luxury as well as the oppression of kings) *and he will take your fields and your olive yards, even the best of them, and give them to his servants; and he will take the tenth of your seed, and of your vineyards, and give them to his officers and to his servants* (by which we see that bribery, corruption, and favoritism are the standing vices of kings) *and he will take the tenth of your men servants, and your maid servants, and your goodliest young men and your asses, and put them to his work; and he will take the tenth of your sheep, and ye shall be his servants, and ye shall cry out in that day because of your king which ye shall have chosen,* AND THE LORD WILL NOT HEAR YOU IN THAT DAY. This accounts for the continuation of monarchy; neither do the characters of the few good kings which have lived since, either sanctify the title, or blot out the sinfulness of the origin; the high encomium given of David takes no notice of him *officially as a king*, but only as a *man* after God's own heart. *Nevertheless the People refused to obey the voice of Samuel, and they said, Nay, but we will have a king over us, that we may be like all the nations, and that our king may judge us, and go out before us and fight our battles.* Samuel continued to reason with them, but to no purpose; he set before them their ingratitude, but all would not avail; and seeing them fully bent on their folly, he cried out, *I will call unto the Lord, and he shall send thunder and rain* (which then was a punishment, being the time of wheat harvest) *that ye may perceive and see that your wickedness is great which ye have done in the sight of the Lord,* IN ASKING YOU A KING. *So Samuel called unto the Lord, and the Lord sent thunder and rain that day, and all the people greatly feared the Lord and Samuel. And all the people said unto Samuel, Pray for thy servants unto the Lord thy God that we die not, for* WE HAVE ADDED UNTO OUR SINS THIS EVIL, TO ASK A KING. These portions of scripture are direct and positive. They admit of no equivocal construction. That the Almighty hath here entered his protest against monarchial government is true, or the scripture is false. And a man hath good reason to believe that there is as much of kingcraft, as priest-craft in withholding the scripture from the public in Popish countries. For monarchy in every instance is the Popery of government.

To the evil of monarchy we have added that of hereditary succession; and as the first is a degradation and lessening of ourselves, so the second, claimed as a matter of right, is an insult and an imposition on posterity. For all men being originally equals, no *one* by *birth* could have a right to set up his own family in perpetual preference to all others for ever, and though himself might deserve *some* decent degree of honors of his contemporaries, yet his descendants might be far too unworthy to inherit them. One of the strongest *natural* proofs of the folly of hereditary right in kings, is, that nature disapproves it, otherwise she would not so frequently turn it into ridicule by giving mankind an *ass for a lion.*

Secondly, as no man at first could possess any other public honors than were bestowed upon him, so the givers of those honors could have no power to give away the right of posterity, and though they might say 'We choose you for *our* head,' they could not, without manifest injustice to their children, say 'that your children and your children's children shall reign over *ours* for ever.' Because such an unwise, unjust, unnatural compact might (perhaps) in the next succession put them under the government of a rogue or a fool. Most wise men, in their private sentiments, have ever treated hereditary right with contempt; yet it is one of those evils, which when once established is not easily removed; many submit from fear, others from superstition, and the more powerful part shares with the king the plunder of the rest.

This is supposing the present race of kings in the world to have had an honourable origin; whereas it is more than probable, that could we take off the dark covering of antiquity, and trace them to their first rise, that we should find the first of them nothing better than the principal ruffian of some restless gang, whose savage manners or pre-eminence in subtilty obtained him the title of chief among plunderers; and who by increasing in power, and extending his depredations, over-awed the quiet and defenceless to purchase their safety by frequent contributions. Yet his electors could have no idea of giving hereditary right to his descendants, because such a perpetual exclusion of themselves was incompatible with the free and unrestrained principles they professed to live by. Wherefore, hereditary succession in the early ages of monarchy could not take place as a matter of claim, but as something casual or complimental; but as few or no records were extant in those days, and traditionary history stuffed with fables, it was very easy, after the lapse of a few generations, to trump up some superstitious tale, conveniently timed, Mahomet like, to cram hereditary right down the throats of the vulgar. Perhaps the disorders which threatened, or seemed to threaten on the decease of a leader and the choice of a new one (for elections among ruffians could not be very orderly) induced many at first to favor hereditary pretentions; by which means it happened, as it hath happened since, that what at first was submitted to as a convenience, was afterwards claimed as a right.

England, since the conquest, hath known some few good monarchs, but groaned beneath a much larger number of bad ones, yet no man in his senses can say that their claim under William the Conqueror is a very honorable one. A French bastard landing with an armed banditti, and establishing himself king of England against the consent of the natives, is in plain terms a very paltry rascally original. – It certainly hath no divinity in it. However, it is needless to spend much time in exposing the folly of hereditary right, if there are any so weak as to believe it, let them promiscuously worship the ass and lion, and welcome. I shall neither copy their humility, nor disturb their devotion.

Yet I should be glad to ask how they suppose kings came at first? The question admits but of three answers, viz. either by lot, by election, or by usurpation. If the first king was taken by lot, it establishes a precedent for the next, which excludes hereditary succession. Saul was by lot yet the succession was not hereditary, neither does it appear from that transaction there was any intention it ever should. If the first king of any country was by election, that likewise establishes a precedent for the next; for to say, that the *right* of all future generations is taken away, by the act of the first electors, in their choice not only of a king, but of a family of kings for ever, hath no parallel in or out of scripture but the doctrine of original sin, which supposes the free will of all men lost in Adam; and from such comparison, and it will admit of no other, hereditary succession can derive no glory. For as in Adam all sinned, and as in the first electors all men obeyed; as in the one all mankind were subjected to Satan, and in the other to Sovereignty; as our innocence was lost in the first, and our authority in the last; and as both disable us from re-assuming some former state and privilege, it unanswerably follows that original sin and hereditary succession are parallels. Dishonourable rank! Inglorious connexion! Yet the most subtile sophist cannot produce a juster simile.

As to usurpation, no man will be so hardy as to defend it; and that William the Conqueror was an usurper is a fact not to be contradicted. The plain truth is, that the antiquity of English monarchy will not bear looking into.

But it is not so much the absurdity as the evil of hereditary succession which concerns mankind. Did it ensure a race of good and wise men it would have the seal of divine authority, but as it opens a door to the *foolish*, the *wicked*, and the *improper*, it hath in it the nature of oppression. Men who look upon themselves born to reign, and others to obey, soon grow insolent; selected from the rest of mankind their minds are early poisoned by importance; and the world they act in differs so materially from the world at large, that they have but little opportunity of knowing its true interests, and when they succeed to the government are frequently the most ignorant and unfit of any throughout the dominions.

Another evil which attends hereditary succession is, that the throne is subject to be possessed by a minor at any age; all which time the regency, acting under the cover of a king, have every opportunity and inducement to betray their trust. The same national misfortune happens, when a king worn out with age and infirmity, enters the last stage of human weakness. In both these cases the public becomes a prey to every miscreant, who can tamper successfully with the follies either of age or infancy.

The most plausible plea, which hath ever been offered in favour of hereditary succession, is, that it preserves a nation from civil wars; and were this true, it would be weighty; whereas, it is the most barefaced falsity ever imposed upon mankind. The whole history of England disowns the fact. Thirty kings and two minors have reigned in that distracted kingdom since the conquest, in which time there have been (including the Revolution) no less than eight civil wars and nineteen rebellions. Wherefore instead of making for peace, it makes against it, and destroys the very foundation it seems to stand on.

The contest for monarchy and succession, between the houses of York and Lancaster, laid England in a scene of blood for many years. Twelve pitched battles, besides skirmishes and sieges, were fought between Henry and Edward. Twice was Henry prisoner to Edward, who in his turn was prisoner to Henry. And so uncertain is the fate of war and the temper of a nation, when nothing but personal matters are the ground of a quarrel, that Henry was taken in triumph from a prison to a palace, and Edward obliged to fly from a palace to a foreign land; yet, as sudden transitions of temper are seldom lasting, Henry in his turn was driven from the throne, and Edward recalled to succeed him. The parliament always following the strongest side.

This contest began in the reign of Henry the Sixth, and was not entirely extinguished till Henry the Seventh, in whom the families were united. Including a period of 67 years, viz. from 1422 to 1489.

In short, monarchy and succession have laid (not this or that kingdom only) but the world in blood and ashes. 'Tis a form of government which the word of God bears testimony against, and blood will attend it.

If we inquire into the business of a king, we shall find that in some countries they have none; and after sauntering away their lives without pleasure to themselves or advantage to the nation, withdraw from the scene, and leave their successors to tread the same idle round. In absolute monarchies the whole weight of business civil and military, lies on the king; the children of Israel in their request for a king, urged this plea 'that he may judge us, and go out before us and fight our battles.' But in countries where he is neither a judge nor a general, as in E—d, a man would be puzzled to know what *is* his business.

The nearer any government approaches to a republic the less business there is for a king. It is somewhat difficult to find a proper name for the government of E—. Sir William Meredith calls it a republic; but in its present state it is unworthy of the name, because the corrupt influence of the crown, by having all the places in its disposal, hath so effectually swallowed up the power, and eaten out the virtue of the house of commons (the republican part in the constitution) that the government of England is nearly as monarchical as that of France or Spain. Men fall out with names without understanding them. For it is the republican and not the monarchical part of the constitution of England which Englishmen glory in, viz. the liberty of choosing an house of commons from out of their own body – and it is easy to see that when the republican virtue fails, slavery ensues. Why is the constitution of E—d sickly, but because monarchy hath poisoned the republic, the crown hath engrossed the commons?

In England a k— hath little more to do than to make war and give away places; which in plain terms, is to impoverish the nation and set it together by the ears. A pretty business indeed for a man to be allowed eight hundred thousand sterling a year for, and worshipped into the bargain! Of more worth is one honest man to society, and in the sight of God, than all the crowned ruffians that ever lived.

THOUGHTS ON THE PRESENT
STATE OF AMERICAN AFFAIRS.

In the following pages I offer nothing more than simple facts, plain arguments, and common sense; and have no other preliminaries to settle with the reader, than that he will divest himself of prejudice and prepossession, and suffer his reason and his feelings to determine for themselves; that he will put *on*, or rather that he will not put *off*, the true character of a man, and generously enlarge his views beyond the present day.

Volumes have been written on the subject of the struggle between England and America. Men of all ranks have embarked in the controversy, from different motives, and with various designs; but all have been ineffectual, and the period of debate is closed. Arms, as the last resource, decide the contest; the appeal was the choice of the king, and the continent hath accepted the challenge.

It hath been reported of the late Mr Pelham

(who tho' an able minister was not without his faults) that on his being attacked in the house of commons, on the score, that his measures were only of a temporary kind, replied, '*they will last my time.*' Should a thought so fatal and unmanly possess the colonies in the present contest, the name of ancestors will be remembered by future generations with detestation.

The sun never shined on a cause of greater worth. 'Tis not the affair of a city, a country, a province, or a kingdom, but of a continent – of at least one eighth part of the habitable globe. 'Tis not the concern of a day, a year, or an age; posterity are virtually involved in the contest, and will be more or less affected, even to the end of time, by the proceedings now. Now is the seed time of continental union, faith and honor. The least fracture now will be like a name engraved with the point of a pin on the tender rind of a young oak; the wound will enlarge with the tree, and posterity read it in full grown characters.

By referring the matter from argument to arms, a new æra for politics is struck; a new method of thinking hath arisen. All plans, proposals, &c. prior to the nineteenth of April, *i. e.* to the commencement of hostilities, are like the almanacks of the last year; which, though proper then, are superceded and useless now. Whatever was advanced by the advocates on either side of the question then, terminated in one and the same point, viz. a union with Great Britain; the only difference between the parties was the method of effecting it; the one proposing force, the other friendship; but it hath so far happened that the first hath failed, and the second hath withdrawn her influence.

As much hath been said of the advantages of reconciliation, which, like an agreeable dream, hath passed away and left us as we were, it is but right, that we should examine the contrary side of the argument, and inquire into some of the many material injuries which these colonies sustain, and always will sustain, by being connected with, and dependant on Great Britain. To examine that connexion and dependance, on the principles of nature and common sense, to see what we have to trust to, if separated, and what we are to expect, if dependant.

I have heard it asserted by some, that as America hath flourished under her former connexion with Great-Britain, that the same connexion is necessary towards her future happiness, and will always have the same effect. Nothing can be more fallacious than this kind of argument. We may as well assert, that because a child has thrived upon milk, that it is never to have meat; or that the first twenty years of our lives is to become a precedent for the next twenty. But even this is admitting more than is true, for I answer roundly, that America would have flourished as much, and probably much more, had no European power had any thing to do with her. The commerce by which she hath enriched herself are the necessaries of life, and will always have a market while eating is the custom of Europe.

But she has protected us, say some. That she hath engrossed us is true, and defended the continent at our expence as well as her own is admitted, and she would have defended Turkey from the same motive, viz. the sake of trade and dominion.

Alas, we have been long led away by ancient prejudices, and made large sacrifices to superstition. We have boasted the protection of Great-Britain, without considering, that her motive was *interest* not *attachment*; that she did not protect us from *our enemies* on *our account*, but from *her enemies* on *her own account*, from those who had no quarrel with us on any *other account*, and who will always be our enemies on the *same account*. Let Britain wave her pretensions to the continent, or the continent throw off the dependance, and we should be at peace with France and Spain were they at war with Britain. The miseries of Hanover last war ought to warn us against connexions.

It hath lately been asserted in parliament, that the colonies have no relation to each other but through the parent country, *i. e.* that Pennsylvania and the Jerseys, and so on for the rest, are sister colonies by the way of England; this is certainly a very round-about way of proving relationship, but it is the nearest and only true way of proving enemyship, if I may so call it. France and Spain never were, nor perhaps ever will be our enemies as *Americans*, but as our being the *subjects of Great Britain*.

But Britain is the parent country, say some. Then the more shame upon her conduct. Even brutes do not devour their young, nor savages make war upon their families; wherefore the assertion, if true, turns to her reproach; but it happens not to be true, or only partly so, and the phrase *parent* or *mother country* hath been jesuitically adopted by the — and his parasites, with a low papistical design of gaining an unfair bias on the credulous weakness of our minds. Europe, and not England, is the parent country of America. This new world hath been the asylum for the persecuted lovers of civil and religious liberty from *every part* of Europe. Hither have they fled, not from the tender embraces of the mother, but from the cruelty of the monster; and it is so far true of England, that the same tyranny which drove the first emigrants from home, pursues their descendants still.

In this extensive quarter of the globe, we forget the narrow limits of three hundred and sixty miles (the extent of England) and carry our friendship on a larger scale; we claim brotherhood with eve-European christian, and triumph in the generosity of the sentiment.

It is pleasant to observe by what regular gradations we surmount the force of local prejudice, as we enlarge our acquaintance with the world. A man born in any town in England divided into parishes, will naturally associate most with his fellow parishioners (because their interests in many cases will be common) and distinguish him by the name of *neighbour*; if he meet him but a few miles from home, he drops the narrow idea of a street, and salutes him by the name of *townsman*; if he travels out of the county, and meet him in any other, he forgets the minor divisions of street and town, and calls him *countryman*, i. e. *countyman*; but if in their foreign excursions they should associate in France or any other part of *Europe*, their local remembrance would be enlarged into that of *Englishmen*. And by a just parity of reasoning, all Europeans meeting in America, or any other quarter of the globe, are *countrymen*; for England, Holland, Germany, or Sweden, when compared with the whole, stand in the same places on the larger scale, which the divisions of street, town, and county do on the smaller ones; distinctions too limited for continental minds. Not one third of the inhabitants, even of this province, are of English descent. Wherefore I reprobate the phrase of parent or mother country applied to England only, as being false, selfish, narrow and ungenerous.

But admitting that we were all of English descent, what does it amount to? Nothing. Britain, being now an open enemy, extinguishes every other name and title: And to say that reconciliation is our duty, is truly farcical. The first king of England, of the present line (William the Conqueror) was a Frenchman, and half the peers of England are descendants from the same country; wherefore by the same method of reasoning, England ought to be governed by France.

Much hath been said of the united strength of Britain and the colonies, that in conjunction they might bid defiance to the world. But this is mere presumption; the fate of war is uncertain, neither do the expressions mean any thing; for this continent would never suffer itself to be drained of inhabitants to support the British arms in either Asia, Africa, or Europe.

Besides, what have we to do with setting the world at defiance? Our plan is commerce, and that, well attended to, will secure us the peace and friendship of all Europe; because it is the interest of all Europe to have America a *free port*. Her trade will always be a protection, and her barrenness of gold and silver secure her from invaders.

I challenge the warmest advocate for reconciliation, to shew, a single advantage that this continent can reap, by being connected with Great Britain. I repeat the challenge, not a single advantage is derived. Our corn will fetch its price in any market in Europe, and our imported goods must be paid for buy them where we will.

But the injuries and disadvantages we sustain by that connection, are without number; and our duty to mankind at large, as well as to ourselves, instruct us to renounce the alliance: Because, any submission to, or dependance on Great Britain, tends directly to involve this continent in European wars and quarrels; and sets us at variance with nations, who would otherwise seek our friendship, and against whom, we have neither anger nor complaint As Europe is our market for trade, we ought to form no partial connection with any part of it. It is the true interest of America to steer clear of European contentions, which she never can do, while by her dependance on Britain, she is made the make-weight in the scale of British politics.

Europe is too thickly planted with kingdoms to be long at peace, and whenever a war breaks out between England and any foreign power, the trade of America goes to ruin, *because of her connection with Britain*. The next war may not turn out like the last, and should it not, the advocates for reconciliation now will be wishing for separation then, because, neutrality in that case, would be a safer convoy than a man of war. Every thing that is right or natural pleads for separation. The blood of the slain, the weeping voice of nature cries, 'TIS TIME TO PART. Even the distance at which the Almighty hath placed England and America, is a strong and natural proof, that the authority of the one, over the other, was never the design of Heaven. The time likewise at which the continent was discovered, adds weight to the argument, and the manner in which it was peopled encreases the force of it. The reformation was preceded by the discovery of America, as if the Almighty graciously meant to open a sanctuary to the persecuted in future years, when home should afford neither friendship nor safety.

The authority of Great-Britain over this continent, is a form of government, which sooner or later must have an end: And a serious mind can draw no true pleasure by looking forward, under the painful and positive conviction, that what he calls 'the present constitution' is merely temporary. As parents, we can have no joy, knowing that *this government* is not sufficiently lasting to ensure any thing which we may bequeath to posterity: And by a plain method of argument, as we are running the next generation into debt, we ought to do the work of it, otherwise we use them meanly and pitifully. In order to discover the line of our duty rightly, we should take our children in our hand, and fix our station a few years farther into life; that eminence will present a prospect, which a few present fears and prejudices conceal from our sight.

Though I would carefully avoid giving unnecessary offence, yet I am inclined to believe, that all those who espouse the doctrine of reconciliation, may be included within the following descriptions. Interested men, who are not to be trusted; weak men who *cannot* see; prejudiced men who *will not* see; and a certain set of moderate men, who think better of the European world than it deserves; and this last class by an ill-judged deliberation, will be the cause of more calamities to this continent than all the other three.

It is the good fortune of many to live distant from the scene of sorrow; the evil is not sufficiently brought to *their* doors to make *them* feel the precariousness with which all American property is possessed. But let our imaginations transport us for a few moments to Boston, that seat of wretchedness will teach us wisdom, and instruct us for ever to renounce a power in whom we can have no trust. The inhabitants of that unfortunate city, who but a few months ago were in ease and affluence, have now no other alternative than to stay and starve, or turn out to beg. Endangered by the fire of their friends if they continue within the city, and plundered by the soldiery if they leave it. In their present condition they are prisoners without the hope of redemption, and in a general attack for their relief, they would be exposed to the fury of both armies.

Men of passive tempers look somewhat lightly over the offences of Britain, and, still hoping for the best, are apt to call out, '*Come we shall be friends again for all this.*' But examine the passions and feelings of mankind. Bring the doctrine of reconciliation to the touchstone of nature, and then tell me, whether you can hereafter love, honour, and faithfully serve the power that hath carried fire and sword into your land? If you cannot do all these, then are you only deceiving yourselves, and by your delay bringing ruin upon posterity. Your future connection with Britain, whom you can neither love nor honour, will be forced and unnatural, and being formed only on the plan of present convenience, will in a little time fall into a relapse more wretched than the first. But if you say, you can still pass the violations over, then I ask, Hath your house been burnt? Hath your property been destroyed before your face? Are your wife and children destitute of a bed to lie on, or bread to live on? Have you lost a parent or a child by their hands, and yourself the ruined and wretched survivor? If you have not, then are you not a judge of those who have. But if you have, and can still shake hands with the murderers, then are you unworthy the name of husband, father, friend, or lover, and whatever may be your rank or title in life, you have the heart of a coward, and the spirit of a sycophant.

This is not inflaming or exaggerating matters, but trying them by those feelings and affections which nature justifies, and without which, we should be incapable of discharging the social duties of life, or enjoying the felicities of it. I mean not to exhibit horror for the purpose of provoking revenge, but to awaken us from fatal and unmanly slumbers, that we may pursue determinately some fixed object. It is not in the power of Britain or of

Europe to conquer America, if she do not conquer herself by *delay* and *timidity*. The present winter is worth an age if rightly employed, but if lost or neglected, the whole continent will partake of the misfortune; and there is no punishment which that man will not deserve, be he who, or what, or where he will, that may be the means of sacrificing a season so precious and useful.

It is repugnant to reason, to the universal order of things, to all examples from the former ages, to suppose, that this continent can longer remain subject to any external power. The most sanguine in Britain does not think so. The utmost stretch of human wisdom cannot, at this time compass a plan short of separation, which can promise the continent even a year's security. Reconciliation is was a falacious dream. Nature hath deserted the connexion, and Art cannot supply her place. For, as Milton wisely expresses, 'never can true reconcilement grow where wounds of deadly hate have pierced so deep.'

Every quiet method for peace hath been ineffectual. Our prayers have been rejected with disdain; and only tended to convince us, that nothing flatters vanity, or confirms obstinacy in Kings more than repeated petitioning – and nothing hath contributed more than that very measure to make the Kings of Europe absolute: Witness Denmark and Sweden. Wherefore since nothing but blows will do, for God's sake, let us come to a final separation, and not leave the next generation to be cutting throats, under the violated unmeaning names of parent and child.

To say, they will never attempt it again is idle and visionary, we thought so at the repeal of the stamp-act, yet a year or two undeceived us; as well we may suppose that nations, which have been once defeated, will never renew the quarrel.

As to government matters, it is not in the power of Britain to do this continent justice: The business of it will soon be too weighty, and intricate, to be managed with any tolerable degree of convenience, by a power, so distant from us, and so very ignorant of us; for if they cannot conquer us, they cannot govern us. To be always running three or four thousand miles with a tale or a petition, waiting four or five months for an answer, which when obtained requires five or six more to explain it in, will in a few years be looked upon as folly and childishness – There was a time when it was proper, and there is a proper time for it to cease.

Small islands not capable of protecting themselves, are the proper objects for kingdoms to take under their care; but there is something very absurd, in supposing a continent to be perpetually governed by an island. In no instance hath nature made the satellite larger than its primary planet, and as England and America, with respect to each other, reverses the common order of nature, it is evident they belong to different systems: England to Europe, America to itself.

I am not induced by motives of pride, party, or resentment to espouse the doctrine of separation and independance; I am clearly, positively, and conscientiously persuaded that it is the true interest of this continent to be so; that every thing short of *that* is mere patchwork, that it can afford no lasting felicity, – that it is leaving the sword to our children, and shrinking back at a time, when, a little more, a little farther, would have rendered this continent the glory of the earth.

As Britain hath not manifested the least inclination towards a compromise, we may be assured that no terms can be obtained worthy the acceptance of the continent, or any ways equal to the expence of blood and treasure we have been already put to.

The object contended for, ought always to bear some just proportion to the expence. The removal of N—, or the whole detestable junto, is a matter unworthy the millions we have expended. A temporary stoppage of trade, was an inconvenience, which would have sufficiently ballanced the repeal of all the acts complained of, had such repeals been obtained; but if the whole continent must take up arms, if every man must be a soldier, it is scarcely worth our while to fight against a contemptible ministry only. Dearly, dearly, do we pay for the repeal of the acts, if that is all we fight for; for in a just estimation, it is as great a folly to pay a Bunker-hill price for law, as for land. As I have always considered the independancy of this continent, as an event, which sooner or later must arrive, so from the late rapid progress of the continent to maturity, the event could not be far off. Wherefore, on the breaking out of hostilities, it was not worth the while to have disputed a matter, which time would have finally redressed, unless we meant to be in earnest; otherwise, it is like wasting an estate on a suit at law, to regulate the trespasses of a tenant, whose lease is just expiring. No man was a warmer wisher for reconciliation than myself, before the fatal nineteenth of April 1775*, but the moment the event of that day was made known, I rejected the hardened, sullen tempered Pharoah of — for ever; and disdain the wretch, that with the pretended title of FATHER OF HIS PEOPLE can unfeelingly hear of their slaughter, and composedly sleep with their blood upon his soul.

But admitting that matters were now made up, what would be the event? I answer, the ruin of the continent. And that for several reasons.

First. The powers of governing still remaining in the hands of the k—, he will have a negative over the whole legislation of this continent. And as he hath shewn himself such an inveterate enemy

---

* *Massacre at Lexington.*

to liberty, and discovered such a thirst for arbitrary power; is he, or is he not, a proper man to say to these colonies, *'You shall make no laws but what I please.'* And is there any inhabitants in America so ignorant, as not to know, that according to what is called the *present constitution*, that this continent can make no laws but what the king gives leave to; and is there any man so unwise, as not to see, that (considering what has happened) he will suffer no Law to be made here, but such as suit his purpose. We may be as effectually enslaved by the want of laws in America, as by submitting to laws made for us in England. After matters are made up (as it is called) can there be any doubt but the whole power of the crown will be exerted, to keep this continent as low and humble as possible? Instead of going forward we shall go backward, or be perpetually quarrelling or ridiculously petitioning. – We are already greater than the king wishes us to be, and will he not hereafter endeavour to make us less? To bring the matter to one point. Is the power who is jealous of our prosperity, a proper power to govern us? Whoever says *No* to this question is an *independant*, for independancy means no more, than, whether we shall make our own laws, or, whether the —, the greatest enemy this continent hath, or can have, shall tell us *'there shall be no laws but such as I like.'*

But the k— you will say has a negative in England; the people there can make no laws without his consent. In point of right and good order, there is something very ridiculous, that a youth of twenty-one (which hath often happened) shall say to several millions of people, older and wiser than himself, I forbid this or that act of yours to be law. But in this place I decline this sort of reply, tho' I will never cease to expose the absurdity of it, and only answer, that England being the king's residence, and America not so, makes quite another case. The k—'s negative *here* is ten times more dangerous and fatal than it can be in England, for *there* he will scarcely refuse his consent to a bill for putting England into as strong a state of defence as possible, and in America he would never suffer such a bill to be passed.

America is only a secondary object in the system of British politics. England consults the good of *this* country, no farther than it answers her *own* purpose. Wherefore, her own interest leads her to suppress the growth of *ours* in every case which doth not promote her advantage, or in the least interfere with it. A pretty state we should soon be in under such a second-hand government, considering what has happened! Men do not change from enemies to friends by the alteration of a name: And in order to shew that reconciliation *now* is a dangerous doctrine, I affirm, *that it would be policy in the k— at this time, to repeal the acts for the sake of reinstating himself in the government of the provinces*; in order, that HE MAY ACCOMPLISH BY

CRAFT AND SUBTILTY, IN THE LONG RUN, WHAT
HE CANNOT DO BY FORCE AND VIOLENCE IN THE
SHORT ONE. Reconciliation and ruin are nearly re-
lated.

Secondly, That as even the best terms, which we
can expect to obtain, can amount to no more than
a temporary expedient, or a kind of government by
guardianship, which can last no longer than till the
colonies come of age, so the general face and state
of things, in the interim, will be unsettled and un-
promising. Emigrants of property will not choose
to come to a country whose form of government
hangs but by a thread, and who is every day tottering on the brink of commotion and disturbance;
and numbers of the present inhabitants would lay
hold of the interval, to dispose of their effects, and
quit the continent.

But the most powerful of all arguments, is, that
nothing but independance, i. e. a continental form
of government, can keep the peace of the continent and preserve it inviolate from civil wars. I
dread the event of a reconciliation with Britain
now, as it is more than probable, that it will be followed by a revolt somewhere or other, the consequences of which may be far more fatal than all
the malice of Britain.

Thousands are already ruined by British barbar-
ity; (thousands more will probably suffer the same
fate.) Those men have other feelings than us who
have nothing suffered. All they *now* possess is lib-

erty, what they before enjoyed is sacrificed to its service, and having nothing more to lose, they disdain submission. Besides, the general temper of the colonies, towards a British government, will be like that of a youth, who is nearly out of his time, they will care very little about her. And a government which cannot preserve the peace, is no government at all, and in that case we pay our money for nothing; and pray what is it that Britain can do, whose power will be wholly on paper, should a civil tumult break out the very day after reconciliation? I have heard some men say, many of whom I believe spoke without thinking, that they dreaded an independance, fearing that it would produce civil wars. It is but seldom that our first thoughts are truly correct, and that is the case here; for there are ten times more to dread from a patched up connexion than from independance. I make the sufferers case my own, and I protest, that were I driven from house and home, my property destroyed, and my circumstances ruined, that as man, sensible of injuries, I could never relish the doctrine of reconciliation, or consider myself bound thereby.

The colonies have manifested such a spirit of good order and obedience to continental government, as is sufficient to make every reasonable person easy and happy on that head. No man can assign the least pretence for his fears, on any other grounds, that such as are truly childish and ridiculous, that one colony will be striving for superiority over another.

Where there are no distinctions there can be no superiority, perfect equality affords no temptation. The republics of Europe are all (and we may say always) in peace. Holland and Swisserland are without wars, foreign or domestic: Monarchical governments, it is true, are never long at rest; the crown itself is a temptation to enterprizing ruffians at *home*; and that degree of pride and insolence ever attendant on regal authority, swells into a rupture with foreign powers, in instances, where a republican government, by being formed on more natural principles, would negociate the mistake.

If there is any true cause of fear respecting independance, it is because no plan is yet laid down. Men do not see their way out – Wherefore, as an opening into that business, I offer the following hints; at the same time modestly affirming, that I have no other opinion of them myself, than that they may be the means of giving rise to something better. Could the straggling thoughts of individuals be collected, they would frequently form materials for wise and able men to improve to useful matter.

LET the assemblies be annual, with a President only. The representation more equal. Their business wholly domestic, and subject to the authority of a Continental Congress.

Let each colony be divided into six, eight, or

ten, convenient districts, each district to send a proper number of delegates to Congress, so that each colony send at least thirty. The whole number in Congress will be at least 390. Each Congress to sit and to choose a president by the following method. When the delegates are met, let a colony be taken from the whole thirteen colonies by lot, after which let the whole Congress choose (by ballot) a president from out of the delegates of *that* province. In the next Congress, let a colony be taken by lot from twelve only, omitting that colony from which the president was taken in the former Congress, and so proceeding on till the whole thirteen shall have had their proper rotation. And in order that nothing may pass into a law but what is satisfactorily just, not less than three fifths of the Congress to be called a majority. – He that will promote discord, under a government so equally formed as this, would join Lucifer in his revolt.

But as there is a peculiar delicacy, from whom, or in what manner, this business must first arise, and as it seems most agreeable and consistent, that it should come from some intermediate body between the governed and the governors, that is between the Congress and the people, let a CONTINENTAL CONFERENCE be held, in the following manner, and for the following purpose.

A committee of twenty-six members of Congress, viz. two for each colony. Two members for each house of assembly, or Provincial convention;

and five representatives of the people at large, to be chosen in the capital city or town of each province, for, and in behalf of the whole province, by as many qualified voters as shall think proper to attend from all parts of the province for that purpose; or, if more convenient, the representatives may be chosen in two or three of the most populous parts thereof. In this conference, thus assembled, will be united, the two grand principles of business, *knowledge* and *power*. The members of Congress, Assemblies, or Conventions, by having had experience in national concerns, will be able and useful counsellors, and the whole, being impowered by the people will have a truly legal authority.

The conferring members being met, let their business be to frame a CONTINENTAL CHARTER, or Charter of the United Colonies; (answering to what is called the Magna Charta of England) fixing the number and manner of choosing members of Congress, members of Assembly, with their date of sitting, and drawing the line of business and jurisdiction between them: (Always remembering, that our strength is continental, not provincial:) Securing freedom and property to all men, and above all things the free exercise of religion, according to the dictates of conscience; with such other matter as is necessary for a charter to contain. Immediately after which, the said conference to dissolve, and the bodies which shall be chosen conformable to the said charter, to be the legislators and governors of this continent for the time being: Whose peace and happiness, may God preserve, Amen.

Should any body of men be hereafter delegated for this or some similar purpose, I offer them the following extracts from that wise observer on governments *Dragonetti*. 'The science' says he, 'of the politician

> consists in fixing the true point of happiness and freedom. Those men would deserve the gratitude of ages, who should discover a mode of government that contained the greatest sum of individual happiness, with the least national expence.
>
> *Dragonetti on Virtue and Rewards.'*

But where says some is the King of America? I'll tell you Friend, he reigns above, and doth not make havock of mankind like the Royal — of Britain. Yet that we may not appear to be defective even in earthly honors, let a day be solemnly set apart for proclaiming the charter; let it be brought forth placed on the divine law, the word of God; let a crown be placed thereon, by which the world may know, that so far as we approve of monarchy, that in America THE LAW IS KING. For as in absolute governments the King is law, so in free countries the law *ought* to be King; and there ought to be no other. But lest any ill use should afterwards arise, let the crown at the conclusion of the ceremony be demolished, and scattered among the people whose right it is.

A government of our own is our natural right: And when a man seriously reflects on the precariousness of human affairs, he will become convinced, that it is infinitely wiser and safer, to form a constitution of our own in a cool deliberate manner, while we have it in our power, than to trust such an interesting event to time and chance. If we omit it now, some *Massenello may hereafter arise, who laying hold of popular disquietudes, may collect together the desperate and the discontented, and by assuming to themselves the powers of government, may sweep away the liberties of the continent like a deluge. Should the government of America return again into the hands of Britain, the tottering situation of things, will be a temptation for some desperate adventurer to try his fortune; and in such a case, what relief can Britain give? Ere she could hear the news the fatal business might be done, and ourselves suffering like the wretched Britons under the oppression of the Conqueror. Ye that oppose independance now, ye know not what ye do; ye are opening a door to eternal tyranny, by keeping vacant the seat of gov-

---

* *Thomas Anello, otherwise Massenello, a fisherman of Naples, who after spiriting up his countrymen in the public market place, against the oppression of the Spaniards, to whom the place was then subject, prompted them to revolt, and in the space of a day became King.*

ernment. There are thousands and tens of thousands, who would think it glorious to expel from the continent, that barbarous and hellish power, which hath stirred up the Indians and Negroes to destroy us; the cruelty hath a double guilt, it is dealing brutally by us, and treacherously by them.

To talk of friendship with those in whom our reason forbids us to have faith, and our affections wounded through a thousand pores instruct us to detest, is madness and folly. Every day wears out the little remains of kindred between us and them, and can there be any reason to hope, that as the relationship expires, the affection will increase, or that we shall agree better, when we have ten times more and greater concerns to quarrel over than ever?

Ye that tell us of harmony and reconciliation, can ye restore to us the time that is past? Can ye give to prostitution its former innocence? Neither can ye reconcile Britain and America. The last cord now is broken, the people of England are presenting addresses against us. There are injuries which nature cannot forgive; she would cease to be nature if she did. As well can the lover forgive the ravisher of his mistress, as the continent forgive the murders of Britain. The Almighty hath implanted in us these unextinguishable feelings for good and wise purposes. They are the guardians of his image in our hearts. They distinguish us from the herd of common animals. The social compact would dissolve, and justice be extirpated the earth, or have only a casual existence were we callous to the touches of affection. The robber and the murderer, would often escape unpunished, did not the injuries which our tempers sustain, provoke us into justice.

O ye that love mankind! Ye that dare oppose, not only the tyranny, but the tyrant, stand forth! Every spot of the old world is over-run with oppression. Freedom hath been hunted round the globe. Asia, and Africa, have long expelled her. – Europe regards her like a stranger, and England hath given her warning to depart. O! receive the fugitive, and prepare in time an asylum for mankind.

▪|||||||||||||||||||||||||||||||||||||||||||||| ▪

OF THE PRESENT
ABILITY OF AMERICA,
WITH SOME MISELLANEOUS
REFLEXIONS.

▪|||||||||||||||||||||||||||||||||||||||||||||| ▪

I have never met with a man, either in England or America, who hath not confessed his opinion, that a separation between the countries, would take place one time or other. And there is no instance in which we have shewn less judgment, than in endeavouring to describe, what we call, the ripeness or fitness of the Continent for independance.

As all men allow the measure, and vary only in their opinion of the time, let us, in order to remove mistakes, take a general survey of things and endeavour if possible, to find out the *very* time. But we need not go far, the inquiry ceases at once, for the *time hath found us*. The general concurrence, the glorious union of all things prove the fact.

It is not in numbers but in unity, that our great strength lies; yet our present numbers are sufficient to repel the force of all the world. The Continent hath, at this time, the largest body of armed and disciplined men of any power under Heaven; and is just arrived at that pitch of strength, in which no single colony is able to support itself, and the whole, when united can accomplish the matter, and either more, or, less than this, might be fatal in its effects. Our land force is already sufficient, and as to naval affairs, we cannot be insensible, that Britain would never suffer an American man of war to be built while the continent remained in her hands. Wherefore we should be no forwarder an hundred years hence in that branch, than we are now; but the truth is, we should be less so, because the timber of the country is every day diminishing, and that which will remain at last, will be far off and difficult to procure.

Were the continent crowded with inhabitants, her sufferings under the present circumstances would be intolerable. The more sea port towns we had, the more should we have both to defend and to loose. Our present numbers are so happily proportioned to our wants, that no man need be idle. The diminution of trade affords an army, and the necessities of an army create a new trade.

Debts we have none; and whatever we may contract on this account will serve as a glorious memento of our virtue. Can we but leave posterity with a settled form of government, an independant constitution of its own, the purchase at any price will be cheap. But to expend millions for the sake

COMMON SENSE | 59

of getting a few vile acts repealed, and routing the present ministry only, is unworthy the charge, and is using posterity with the utmost cruelty; because it is leaving them the great work to do, and a debt upon their backs, from which they derive no advantage. Such a thought is unworthy a man of honor, and is the true characteristic of a narrow heart and a pedling politician.

The debt we may contract doth not deserve our regard if the work be but accomplished. No nation ought to be without a debt. A national debt is a national bond; and when it bears no interest, is in no case a grievance. Britain is oppressed with a debt of upwards of one hundred and forty millions sterling, for which she pays upwards of four millions interest. And as a compensation for her debt, she has a large navy; America is without a debt, and without a navy; yet for the twentieth part of the English national debt, could have a navy as large again. The navy of England is not worth, at this time, more than three millions and a half sterling.

The first and second editions of this pamphlet were published without the following calculations, which are now given as a proof that the above estimation of the navy is a just one. *See Entic's naval history, intro.* page 56.

The charge of building a ship of each rate, and furnishing her with masts, yards, sails and rigging, together with a proportion of eight months boatswain's and carpenter's sea-stores, as calculated by Mr Burchett, Secretary to the navy.

	£.
For a ship of 100 guns	35,553
90	29,886
80	23,638
70	17,785
60	14,197
50	10,606
40	7,558
30	5,846
20	3,710

And from hence it is easy to sum up the value, or cost rather, of the whole British navy, which in the year 1757, when it was as its greatest glory consisted of the following ships and guns:

Ships.	Guns.	Cost of one.	Cost of all.
6	100	35,553 *l.*	213,318 *l.*
12	90	29,886	358,632
12	80	23,638	283,656
43	70	17,785	746,755
35	60	14,197	496,895
40	50	10,606	424,240
45	40	7,558	340,110
58	20	3,710	215,180
85 Sloops, bombs, and fireships, one with another, at		2,000	170,000

	Cost 3,266,786
Remains for guns, -----	233,214
	Total, 3,500,000

No country on the globe is so happily situated, so internally capable of raising a fleet as America. Tar, timber, iron, and cordage are her natural produce. We need go abroad for nothing. Whereas the Dutch, who make large profits by hiring out their ships of war to the Spaniards and Portuguese, are obliged to import most of the materials they use. We ought to view the building a fleet as an article of commerce, it being the natural manufactory of this country. It is the best money we can lay out. A navy when finished is worth more than it cost. And is that nice point in national policy, in which commerce and protection are united. Let us build; if we want them not, we can sell; and by that means replace our paper currency with ready gold and silver.

In point of manning a fleet, people in general run into great errors; it is not necessary that one-fourth part should be sailors. The Terrible privateer, Captain Death, stood the hottest engagement of any ship last war, yet had not twenty sailors on board, though her complement of men was upwards of two hundred. A few able and social sailors will soon instruct a sufficient number of active land-men in the common work of a ship. Wherefore, we never can be more capable to begin on maritime matters than now, while our timber is standing, our fisheries blocked up, and our sailors and shipwrights out of employ. Men of war of seventy and 80 guns were built forty years ago in

New-England, and why not the same now? Ship-building is America's greatest pride, and in which, she will in time excel the whole world. The great empires of the east are mostly inland, and consequently excluded from the possibility of rivalling her. Africa is in a state of barbarism; and no power in Europe, hath either such an extent or coast, or such an internal supply of materials. Where nature hath given the one, she has withheld the other; to America only hath she been liberal of both. The vast empire of Russia is almost shut out from the sea; wherefore, her boundless forests, her tar, iron, and cordage are only articles of commerce.

In point of safety, ought we to be without a fleet? We are not the little people now, which we were sixty years ago; at that time we might have trusted our property in the streets, or fields rather; and slept securely without locks or bolts to our doors or windows. The case now is altered, and our methods of defence ought to improve with our increase of property. A common pirate, twelve months ago, might have come up the Delaware, and laid the city of Philadelphia under instant contribution, for what sum he pleased; and the same might have happened to other places. Nay, any daring fellow, in a brig of fourteen or sixteen guns, might have robbed the whole Continent, and carried off half a million of money. These are circumstances which demand our attention, and point out the necessity of naval protection.

Some, perhaps, will say, that after we have made it up with Britain, she will protect us. Can we be so unwise as to mean, that she shall keep a navy in our harbours for that purpose? Common sense will tell us, that the power which hath endeavoured to subdue us, is of all others the most improper to defend us. Conquest may be effected under the pretence of friendship; and ourselves, after a long and brave resistance, be at last cheated into slavery. And if her ships are not to be admitted into our harbours, I would ask, how is she to protect us? A navy three or four thousand miles off can be of little use, and on sudden emergencies, none at all. Wherefore, if we must hereafter protect ourselves, why not do it for ourselves? Why do it for another?

The English list of ships of war is long and formidable, but not a tenth part of them are at any one time fit for service, numbers of them not in being; yet their names are pompously continued in the list, if only a plank be left of the ship: and not a fifth part, of such as are fit for service, can be spared on any one station at one time. The East, and West Indies, Mediterranean, Africa, and other parts over which Britain extends her claim, make large demands upon her navy. From a mixture of prejudice and inattention, we have contracted a false notion respecting the navy of England, and have talked as if we should have the whole of it to encounter at once, and for that reason, supposed that we must have one as large; which not being instantly practicable, have been made use of by a set of disguised Tories to discourage our beginning thereon. Nothing can be farther from truth than this; for if America had only a twentieth part of the naval force of Britain, she would be by far an over match for her; because, as we neither have, nor claim any foreign dominion, our whole force would be employed on our own coast, where we should, in the long run, have two to one the advantage of those who had three or four thousand miles to sail over, before they could attack us, and the same distance to return in order to refit and recruit. And although Britain by her fleet, hath a check over our trade to Europe, we have as large a one over her trade to the West-Indies, which, by laying in the neighbourhood of the Continent, is entirely at its mercy.

Some method might be fallen on to keep up a naval force in time of peace, if we should not judge it necessary to support a constant navy. If premiums were to be given to merchants, to build and employ in their service, ships mounted with twenty, thirty, forty, or fifty guns, (the premiums to be in proportion to the loss of bulk to the merchants) fifty or sixty of those ships, with a few guard ships on constant duty, would keep up a sufficient navy, and that without burdening ourselves with the evil so loudly complained of in England, of suffering their fleet, in time of peace to lie rotting in the docks. To unite the sinews of commerce and defence is sound policy; for when our strength and our riches, play into each other's hand, we need fear no external enemy.

In almost every article of defence we abound. Hemp flourishes even to rankness, so that we need not want cordage. Our iron is superior to that of other countries. Our small arms equal to any in the world. Cannon we can cast at pleasure. Saltpetre and gunpowder we are every day producing. Our knowledge is hourly improving. Resolution is our inherent character, and courage hath never yet forsaken us. Wherefore, what is it that we want? Why is it that we hesitate? From Britain we can expect nothing but ruin. If she is once admitted to the government of America again, this Continent will not be worth living in. Jealousies will be always arising; insurrections will be constantly happening; and who will go forth to quell them? Who will venture his life to reduce his own countrymen to a foreign obedience? The difference between Pennsylvania and Connecticut, respecting some unlocated lands, shews the insignificance of a B—sh government, and fully proves, that nothing but Continental authority can regulate Continental matters.

Another reason why the present time is preferable to all others, is, that the fewer our numbers are, the more land there is yet unoccupied, which instead of being lavished by the k—on his worthless dependants, may be hereafter applied, not only to the discharge of the present debt, but to the constant support of government. No nation under heaven hath such an advantage as this.

The infant state of the Colonies, as it is called, so far from being against, is an argument in favor of independance. We are sufficiently numerous, and were we more so, we might be less united. It is a matter worthy of observation, that the more a country is peopled, the smaller their armies are. In military numbers, the ancients far exceeded the moderns: and the reason is evident, for trade being the consequence of population, men become too much absorbed thereby to attend to any thing else. Commerce diminishes the spirit, both of patriotism and military defence. And history sufficiently informs us, that the bravest achievements were always accomplished in the non-age of a nation. With the increase of commerce, England hath lost its spirit. The city of London, notwithstanding its numbers, submits to continued insults with the patience of a coward. The more men have to lose, the less willing are they to venture. The rich are in general slaves to fear, and submit to courtly power with the trembling duplicity of a spaniel.

Youth is the seed time of good habits, as well in nations as in individuals. It might be difficult, if not impossible, to form the Continent into one government half a century hence. The vast variety of interests, occasioned by an increase of trade and population, would create confusion. Colony would be against colony. Each being able might scorn each other's assistance: and while the proud and foolish gloried in their little distinctions, the wise would lament that the union had not been formed before. Wherefore, the *present time* is the *true time* for establishing it. The intimacy which is contracted in infancy, and the friendship which is formed in misfortune, are, of all others, the most lasting and unalterable. Our present union is marked with both these characters: we are young, and we have been distressed; but our concord hath withstood our troubles, and fixes a memorable æra for posterity to glory in.

The present time, likewise, is that peculiar time, which never happens to a nation but once, *viz.* the time of forming itself into a government. Most nations have let slip the opportunity, and by that means have been compelled to receive laws from their conquerors, instead of making laws for themselves. First, they had a king, and then a form of government; whereas, the articles or charter of government, should be formed first, and men delegated to execute them afterward: but from the errors of other nations, let us learn wisdom, and lay hold of the present opportunity – *To begin government at the right end.*

When William the conqueror subdued England he gave them law at the point of the sword; and until we consent that the seat of government in America, be legally and authoritatively occupied, we shall be in danger of having it filled by some fortunate ruffian, who may treat us in the same manner, and then, where will be our freedom? where our property?

As to religion, I hold it to be the indispensible duty of all government, to protect all conscientious professors thereof, and I know of no other business which government hath to do therewith. Let a man throw aside that narrowness of soul, that selfishness of principle, which the niggards of all professions are so unwilling to part with, and he will be at once delivered of his fears on that head. Suspicion is the companion of mean souls, and the bane of all good society. For myself I fully and conscientiously believe, that it is the will of the Almighty, that there should be diversity of religious opinions among us: It affords a larger field for our christian kindness. Were we all of one way of thinking, our religious dispositions would want matter for probation; and on this liberal principle, I look on the various denominations among us, to be like children of the same family, differing only, in what is called their Christian names.

In page fifty-four,* I threw out a few thoughts on the propriety of a Continental Charter, (for I only presume to offer hints, not plans) and in this place, I take the liberty of rementioning the sub-

---

* [Page 52 in this edition.]

ject, by observing, that a charter is to be understood as a bond of solemn obligation, which the whole enters into, to support the right of every separate part, whether of religion, personal freedom, or property, A firm bargain and a right reckoning make long friends.

In a former page I likewise mentioned the necessity of a large and equal representation; and there is no political matter which more deserves our attention. A small number of electors, or a small number of representatives, are equally dangerous. But if the number of the representatives be not only small, but unequal, the danger is increased. As an instance of this, I mention the following; when the Associators petition was before the House of Assembly of Pennsylvania; twenty-eight members only were present, all the Bucks county members, being eight, voted against it, and had seven of the Chester members done the same, this whole province had been governed by two counties only, and this danger it is always exposed to. The unwarrantable stretch likewise, which that house made in their last sitting, to gain an undue authority over the Delegates of that province, ought to warn the people at large, how they trust power out of their own hands. A set of instructions for the Delegates were put together, which in point of sense and business would have dishonored a school-boy, and after being approved by a *few*, a *very few* without doors, were carried

tions, be considered as rebels. The precedent is somewhat dangerous to *their peace*, for men to be in arms under the name of subjects; we on the spot, can solve the paradox: but to unite resistance and subjection, requires an idea much too refined for common understanding.

Fourthly. – Were a manifesto to be published, and despatched to foreign courts, setting forth the miseries we have endured, and the peaceable methods we have ineffectually used for redress; declaring, at the same time, that not being able, any longer to live happily or safely under the cruel disposition of the B—sh court, we had been driven to the necessity of breaking off all connection with her; at the same time assuring all such courts of our peaceable disposition towards them, and of our desire of entering into trade with them: Such a memorial would produce more good effects to this Continent, than if a ship were freighted with petitions to Britain.

Under our present denomination of British subjects we can neither be received nor heard abroad: The custom of all courts is against us, and will be so, until, by an independance, we take rank with other nations.

These proceedings may at first appear strange and difficult; but, like all other steps which we have already passed over, will in a little time become familiar and agreeable; and, until an independance is declared, the Continent will feel itself

like a man who continues putting off some un-
pleasant business from day to day, yet knows it
must be done, hates to set about it, wishes it over,
and is continually haunted with the thoughts of its
necessity.

S ince the publication of the first edition of
this pamphlet, or rather, on the same day on
which it came out, the —'s Speech made its
appearance in this city. Had the spirit of prophecy
directed the birth of this production, it could not
have brought it forth, at a more seasonable junc-
ture, or a more necessary time. The bloody mind-
edness of the one, shew the necessity of pursuing
the doctrine of the other. Men read by way of
revenge. And the speech instead of terrifying,
prepared a way for the manly principles of Independance.

Ceremony, and even, silence, from whatever
motive they may arise, have a hurtful tendency,
when they give the least degree of countenance to
base and wicked performances; wherefore, if this
maxim be admitted, it naturally follows, that the
—'s speech, as being a piece of finished villainy, de-

served, and still deserves, a general execration both by the Congress and the people. Yet as the domestic tranquility of a nation, depends greatly on the *chastity* of what may properly be called NATIONAL MATTERS, it is often better, to pass some things over in silent disdain, than to make use of such new methods of dislike, as might introduce the least innovation, on that guardian of our peace and safety. And perhaps, it is chiefly owing to this prudent delicacy, that the —'s Speech, hath not before now, suffered a public execution. The Speech if it may be called one, is nothing better than a wilful audacious libel against the truth, the common good, and the existence of mankind; and is a formal and pompous method of offering up human sacrifices to the pride of tyrants. But this general massacre of mankind, is one of the privileges, and the certain consequences of K—s; for as nature knows them *not*, they know *not her*, and although they are beings of our *own* creating, they know not *us*, and are become the gods of their creators. The speech hath one good quality, which is, that it is not calculated to deceive, neither can we, even if we would, be deceived by it. Brutality and tyranny appear on the face of it. It leaves us at no loss: And every line convinces, even in the moment of reading, that He, who hunts the woods for prey, the naked and untutored Indian, is less a Savage than the — of B—.

Sir J—n D—e, the putative father of a whining

jesuitical piece, fallaciously called, '*The Address of the people of* ENGLAND *to the inhabitants of* AMERICA,' hath, perhaps from a vain supposition, that the people *here* were to be frightened at the pomp and description of a king, given, (though very unwisely on his part) the real character of the present one: 'But,' says this writer, 'if you are inclined to pay compliments to an administration, which we do not complain of,' (meaning the Marquis of Rockingham's at the repeal of the Stamp Act) 'it is very unfair in you to withold them from that prince, *by whose* NOD ALONE *they were permitted to do any thing.*' this is toryism with a witness! Here is idolatry even without a mask: And he who can calmly hear, and digest such doctrine, hath forfeited his claim to rationality – an apostate from the order of manhood; and ought to be considered – as one, who hath, not only given up the proper dignity of a man, but sunk himself beneath the rank of animals, and contemptibly crawl through the world like a worm.

However, it matters very little now, what the — of E— either says or does; he hath wickedly broken through every moral and human obligation, trampled nature and conscience beneath his feet; and by a steady and constitutional spirit of insolence and cruelty, procured for himself an universal hatred. It is *now* the interest of America to provide for herself. She hath already a large and young family, whom it is more her duty to take care of, than to be granting away her property, to support a power who is become a reproach to the names of men and christians – ye, whose office it is to watch over the morals of a nation, of whatsoever sect or denomination ye are of, as well as ye, who are more immediately the guardians of the public liberty, if ye wish to preserve your native country uncontaminated by European corruption, ye must in secret wish a separation – But leaving the moral part to private reflection, I shall chiefly confine my farther remarks to the following heads.

First, That it is the interest of America to be separated from Britain.

Secondly. Which is the easiest and most practicable plan, RECONCILIATION or INDEPENDANCE? with some occasional remarks.

In support of the first, I could, if I judged it proper, produce the opinion of some of the ablest and most experienced men on this continent; and whose sentiments, on that head, are not yet publickly known. It is in reality a self-evident position: For no nation in a state of foreign dependance, limited in its commerce, and cramped and fettered in its legislative powers, can ever arrive at any material eminence. America doth not yet know what opulence is; and although the progress which she hath made stands unparalleled in the history of other nations, it is but childhood, compared with what she would be capable of arriving at, had she, as she ought to have, the legislative powers in her own hands. England is, at this time, proudly coveting what would do her no good, were she to accomplish it; and the Continent hesitating on a matter, which will be her final ruin if neglected. It is the commerce and not the conquest of America, by which England is to be benefited, and that would in a great measure continue, were the countries as independant of each other as France and Spain; because in many articles, neither can go to a better market. But it is the independance of this country on Britain or any other, which is now the main and only object worthy of contention, and which, like all other truths discovered by necessity, will appear clearer and stronger every day.

First. Because it will come to that one time or other.

Secondly. Because the longer it is delayed the harder it will be to accomplish.

I have frequently amused myself both in public and private companies, with silently remarking the spacious errors of those who speak without reflecting. And among the many which I have heard, the following seems the most general, viz. that had this rupture happened forty or fifty years hence, instead of *now*, the Continent would have been more able to have shaken off the dependance. To which I reply, that our military ability *at this time*, arises from the experience gained in the last war, and which in forty or fifty years time, would have been totally extinct. The Continent, would not, by that time, have had a General, or even a military officer left; and we, or those who may succeed us, would have been as ignorant of martial matters as the ancient Indians: And this single position, closely attended to, will unanswerably prove, that the present time is preferable to all others: The argument turns thus – at the conclusion of the last war, we had experience, but wanted numbers; and forty or fifty years hence, we should have numbers, without experience; wherefore, the proper point of time, must be some particular point between the two extremes, in which a sufficiency of the former remains, and a proper increase of the latter is obtained: And that point of time is the present time.

The reader will pardon this digression, as it does not properly come under the head I first set out with, and to which I again return by the following position, viz.

Should affairs be patched up with Britain, and she to remain the governing and sovereign power of America, (which as matters are now circumstanced, is giving up the point entirely) we shall deprive ourselves of the very means of sinking the debt we have or may contract. The value of the back lands which some of the provinces are clandestinely deprived of, by the unjust extention of the limits of Canada, valued only at five pounds sterling per hundred acres, amount to upwards of twenty-five millions, Pennsylvania currency; and the quit-rents at one penny sterling per acre, to two millions yearly.

It is by the sale of those lands that the debt may be sunk, without burthen to any, and the quit-rent reserved thereon, will always lessen, and in time, will wholly support the yearly expence of government. It matters not how long the debt is in paying, so that the lands when sold be applied to the discharge of it, and for the execution of which, the Congress for the time being, will be the continental trustees.

I proceed now to the second head, viz. Which is the earliest and most practicable plan, RECONCILI-ATION or INDEPENDANCE? with some occasional remarks.

He who takes nature for his guide is not easily beaten out of his argment, and on that ground, I answer generally – *That* INDEPENDANCE *being a* SINGLE SIMPLE LINE, *contained within ourselves; and reconciliation, a matter exceedingly perplexed and complicated, and in which, a treacherous capricious court is to interfere, gives the answer without a doubt.*

The present state of America is truly alarming to every man who is capable of reflexion. Without law, without government, without any other mode of power than what is founded on, and granted by courtesy. Held together by an unexampled concurrence of sentiment, which is nevertheless subject to change, and which every secret enemy is endeavouring to dissolve. Our present condition, is,

Legislation without law; wisdom without a plan; a
constitution without a name; and, what is strangely
astonishing, perfect Independance contending for
Dependance. The instance is without a precedent;
the case never existed before; and who can tell
what may be the event? The property of no man is
secure in the present unbraced system of things.
The mind of the multitude is left at random, and
feeling no fixed object before them, they pursue
such as fancy or opinion starts. Nothing is crimi-
nal; there is no such thing as treason; wherefore,
every one thinks himself at liberty to act as he
pleases. The Tories dared not to have assembled of-
fensively, had they known that their lives, by that
act were forfeited to the laws of the state. A line of
distinction should be drawn, between English soldiers taken in battle, and inhabitants of America
taken in arms. The first are prisoners, but the latter
traitors. The one forfeits his liberty the other his
head.

Notwithstanding our wisdom, there is a visible
feebleness in some of our proceedings which gives
encouragement to dissentions. The Continental
belt is too loosely buckled. And if something is not
done in time, it will be too late to do any thing,
and we shall fall into a state, in which, neither *reconciliation* nor *independance* will be practicable. The
— and his worthless adherents are got at their old
game of dividing the Continent, and there are not
wanting among us, Printers, who will be busy

spreading specious falsehoods. The artful and hyp-ocritical letter which appeared a few months ago in two of the New-York papers, and likewise in two others, is an evidence that there are men who want either judgement or honesty.

It is easy getting into holes and corners and talking of reconciliation: But do such men seri-ously consider, how difficult the task is, and how dangerous it may prove, should the Continent di-vide thereon. Do they take within their view, all the various orders of men whose situation and cir-cumstances, as well as their own, are to be consid-ered therein. Do they put themselves in the place of the sufferer whose *all* is *already* gone, and of the soldier, who hath quitted *all* for the defence of his country. If their ill-judged moderation be suited to their own private situations *only*, regardless of oth-ers, the event will convince them, that 'they are reckoning without their Host.'

Put us, says some, on the footing we were on in sixty-three: To which I answer, the request is not *now* in the power of Britain to comply with, nei-ther will she propose it; but if it were, and even should be granted, I ask, as a reasonable question, By what means is such a corrupt and faithless court to be kept to its engagements? Another par-liament, nay, even the present, may hereafter repeal the obligation, on the pretence of its being vio-lently obtained, or unwisely granted; and in that case, Where is our redress? – No going to law with nations; cannon are the barristers of crowns; and the sword, not of justice, but of war, decides the suit. To be on the footing of sixty-three, it is not sufficient, that the laws only be put on the same state, but, that our circumstances, likewise, be put on the same state; our burnt and destroyed towns repaired or built up, our private losses made good, our public debts (contracted for defence) discharged; otherwise, we shall be millions worse than we were at that enviable period. Such a request had it been complied with a year ago, would have won the heart and soul of the Continent – but now it is too late, 'The Rubicon is passed.'

Besides the taking up arms, merely to enforce the repeal of a pecuniary law, seems as unwarrantable by the divine law, and as repugnant to human feelings, as the taking up arms to enforce obedience thereto. The object, on either side, doth not justify the ways and means; for the lives of men are too valuable to be cast away on such trifles. It is the violence which is done and threatened to our persons; the destruction of our property by an armed force; the invasion of our country by fire and sword, which conscientiously qualifies the use of arms: And the instant, in which such a mode of defence became necessary, all subjection to Britain ought to have ceased; and the independancy of America should have been considered, as dating its æra from, and published by, *the first musket that was fired against her*. This line is a line of consistency;

neither drawn by caprice, nor extended by ambition; but produced by a chain of events, of which the colonies were not the authors.

I shall conclude these remarks, with the following timely and well Intended hints, We ought to reflect, that there are three different ways by which an independancy may hereafter be effected; and that *one* of those *three*, will one day or other, be the fate of America, viz. By the legal voice of the people in Congress; by a military power; or by a mob: It may not always happen that our soldiers are citizens, and the multitude a body of reasonable men; virtue, as I have already remarked, is not hereditary, neither is it perpetual. Should an independancy be brought about by the first of those means, we have every opportunity and every encouragement before us, to form the noblest, purest constitution on the face of the earth. We have it in our power to begin the world over again. A situation, similar to the present, hath not happened since the days of Noah until now. The birth-day of a new world is at hand, and a race of men perhaps as numerous as all Europe contains, are to receive their portion of freedom from the event of a few months. The Reflexion is awful – and in this point of view, How trifling, how ridiculous, do the little, paltry cavellings, of a few weak or interested men appear, when weighed against the business of a world.

Should we neglect the present favorable and inviting period, and an independance be hereafter effected by any other means, we must charge the consequence to ourselves, or to those rather, whose narrow and prejudiced souls, are habitually opposing the measure, without either inquiring or reflecting. There are reasons to be given in support of Independence, which men should rather privately think of, than be publicly told of. We ought not now to be debating whether we shall be independant or not, but, anxious to accomplish it on a firm, secure, and honorable basis, and uneasy rather that it is not yet began upon. Every day convinces us of its necessity. Even the Tories (if such beings yet remain among us) should, of all men, be the most solicitous to promote it; for, as the appointment of committees at first, protected them from popular rage, so, a wise and well established form of government, will be the only certain means of continuing it securely to them. *Wherefore*, if they have not virtue enough to be WHIGS, they ought to have prudence enough to wish for Independence.

In short, Independance is the only BOND that can tye and keep us together. We shall then see our object, and our ears will be legally shut against the schemes of an intriguing, as well as a cruel enemy. We shall then too, be on a proper footing, to treat with Britain; for there is reason to conclude, that the pride of that court, will be less hurt by treating with the American states for terms of peace, than with those, whom she denominates, 'rebellious subjects,' for terms of accommodation. It is our delaying it that encourages her to hope for conquest, and our backwardness tends only to prolong the war. As we have, without any good effect therefrom, with-held our trade to obtain a redress of our grievances, let us *now* try the alternative, by *independantly* redressing them ourselves, and then offering to open the trade. The mercantile and reasonable part of England will be still with us; because, peace *with* trade, is preferable to war *without* it. And if this offer be not accepted, other courts may be applied to.

On these grounds I rest the matter. And as no offer hath yet been made to refute the doctrine contained in the former editions of this pamphlet, it is a negative proof, that either the doctrine cannot be refuted, or, that the party in favour of it are too numerous to be opposed. Wherefore, instead of gazing at each other with suspicious or doubtful curiosity, let each of us, hold out to his neighbour the hearty hand of friendship, and unite in drawing a line, which, like an act of oblivion, shall bury in forgetfulness every former dissention. Let the names of Whig and Tory be extinct; and let none other be heard among us, than those of *a good citizen, an open and resolute friend, and a virtuous supporter of the* RIGHTS *of* MANKIND *and of the* FREE AND INDEPENDANT STATES OF AMERICA.

*

*To the Representatives of the Religious Society of the
People called Quakers, or to so many of them as were
concerned in publishing a late piece, entitled 'The Ancient Testimony and Principles of the people called
Quakers renewed, with respect to the King and Government, and Touching the Commotions now prevail-
ing in these and other parts of America, addressed to
the people in general.*

The Writer of this, is one of those few, who never
dishonors religion either by ridiculing, or cavilling
at any denomination whatsoever. To God, and not
to man, are all men accountable on the score of
religion. Wherefore, this epistle is not so properly
addressed to you as a religious, but as a political
body, dabbling in matters, which the professed
Quietude of your Principles instruct you not to
meddle with.

As you have, without a proper authority for so
doing, put yourselves in the place of the whole
body of the Quakers, so, the writer of this, in order
to be on an equal rank with yourselves, is under the
necessity, of putting himself in the place of all
those who approve the very writings and principles, against which your testimony is directed: And
he hath chosen their singular situation, in order
that you might discover in him, that presumption
of character which you cannot see in yourselves.

For neither he nor you have any claim or title to *Political Representation*.

When men have departed from the right way, it is no wonder that they stumble and fall. And it is evident from the manner in which ye have managed your testimony, that politics, (as a religious body of men) is not your proper Walk; for however well adapted it might appear to you, it is, nevertheless, a jumble of good and bad put unwisely together, and the conclusion drawn therefrom, both unnatural and unjust.

The two first pages, (and the whole doth not make four) we give you credit for, and expect the same civility from you, because the love and desire of peace is not confined to Quakerism, it is the *natural*, as well as the religious wish of all denominations of men. And on this ground, as men labouring to establish an Independant Constitution of our own, do we exceed all others in our hope, end, and aim. *Our plan is peace for ever.* We are tired of contention with Britain, and can see no real end to it but in a final separation. We act consistently, because for the sake of introducing an endless and uninterrupted peace, do we bear the evils and burthens of the present day. We are endeavouring, and will steadily continue to endeavor, to separate and dissolve a connexion which hath already filled our land with blood; and which, while the name of it remains, will be the fatal cause of future mischiefs to both countries.

We fight neither for revenge nor conquest; neither from pride nor passion; we are not insulting the world with our fleets and armies, nor ravaging the globe for plunder. Beneath the shade of our own vines are we attacked; in our own houses, and on our own lands, is the violence committed against us. We view our enemies in the characters of Highwaymen and Housebreakers, and having no defence for ourselves in the civil law, are obliged to punish them by the military one, and apply the sword, in the very case, where you have before now, applied the halter. – Perhaps we feel for the ruined and insulted sufferers in all and every part of the continent, and with a degree of tenderness which hath not yet made its way into some of your bosoms. But be ye sure that ye mistake not the cause and ground of your Testimony. Call not coldness of soul, religion; nor put the *Bigot* in the place of the *Christian*.

O ye partial ministers of your own acknowledged principles. If the bearing arms be sinful, the first going to war must be more so, by all the difference between wilful attack and unavoidable defence. Wherefore, if ye really preach from conscience, and mean not to make a political hobby-horse of your religion, convince the world thereof, by proclaiming your doctrine to our enemies, *for they likewise bear* ARMS. Give us proof of your sincerity by publishing it at St. James's, to the commanders in chief at Boston, to the Admirals and Captains who are piratically ravaging our coasts, and to all the murdering miscreants who are acting in authority under him whom ye profess to serve. Had ye the honest soul of *Barclay ye would preach repentance to *your* king; Ye would tell the Royal — his sins, and warn him of eternal ruin. Ye would not spend your partial invectives against the injured and the insulted only, but like faithful ministers, would cry aloud and *spare none*. Say not that ye are persecuted, neither endeavour to make us the authors of that reproach, which, ye are bringing upon yourselves; for we testify unto all men, that we do not complain against you because ye are *Quakers*, but because ye pretend to *be* and are NOT Quakers.

Alas! it seems by the particular tendency of some part of your testimony, and other parts of your conduct, as if all sin was reduced to, and comprehended in *the act of bearing arms*, and that by

---

* *'Thou hast tasted of prosperity and adversity; thou knowest what it is to be banished thy native country, to be over-ruled as well as to rule, and set upon the throne; and being oppressed thou hast reason to know now hateful the oppressor is both to God and man: If after all these warnings and advertisements, thou dost not turn unto the Lord with all thy heart, but forget him who remembered thee in thy distress, and give up thyself to follow lust and vanity, surely great will be thy condemnation.—Against which snare, as well as the temptation of those who may or do feed thee, and prompt thee to evil, the most excellent and prevalent remedy will be, to apply thyself to that light of Christ which shineth in thy conscience and which neither can, nor will flatter thee, nor suffer thee to be at ease in thy sins.'*

Barclay's Address to Charles II.

the *people only*. Ye appear to us, to have mistaken party for conscience, because the general tenor of your actions wants uniformity: And it is exceedingly difficult to us to give credit to many of your pretended scruples; because we see them made by the same men, who, in the very instant that they are exclaiming against the mammon of this world, are nevertheless, hunting after it with a step as steady as Time, and an appetite as keen as Death.

The quotation which ye have made from Proverbs, in the third page of your testimony, that, 'when a man's ways please the Lord, he maketh even his enemies to be at peace with him'; is very unwisely chosen on your part; because it amounts to a proof, that the king's ways (whom ye are so desirous of supporting) do *not* please the Lord, otherwise, his reign would be in peace.

I now proceed to the latter part of your testimony, and that, for which all the foregoing seems only an introduction, viz.

'It hath ever been our judgment and principle, since we were called to profess the light of Christ Jesus, manifested in our consciences unto this day, that the setting up and putting down kings and governments, is God's peculiar prerogative; for causes best known to himself: And that it is not our business to have any hand or contrivance therein; nor to be busy bodies above our station, much less to plot and contrive the ruin, or overturn any of them, but to pray for the king, and safety of our nation, and good of all men: That we may live a peaceable and quiet life, in all goodliness and honesty; *under the government which God is pleased to set over us.'* – If these are *really* your principles why do ye not abide by them? Why do ye not leave that, which ye call God's Work, to be managed by himself? These very principles instruct you to wait with patience and humility, for the event of all public measures, and to receive *that event* as the divine will towards you. *Wherefore*, what occasion is there for your *political testimony* if you fully believe what it contains? And the very publishing it proves, that either, ye do not believe what ye profess, or have not virtue enough to practise what ye believe.

The principles of Quakerism have a direct tendency to make a man the quiet and inoffensive subject of any, and every government *which is set over him*. And if the setting up and putting down of kings and governments is God's peculiar prerogative, he most certainly will not be robbed thereof by us; wherefore, the principle itself leads you to approve of every thing, which ever happened, or may happen to kings as being his work, OLIVER CROMWELL thanks you. – CHARLES, then, died not by the hands of man; and should the present Proud Imitator of him, come to the same untimely end, the writers and publishers of the testimony, are bound by the doctrine it contains, to applaud the fact. Kings are not taken away by miracles, neither are changes in governments brought about by any other means than such as are common and human; and such as we are now using. Even the dispersing of the Jews, though foretold by our Saviour, was effected by arms. Wherefore, as ye refuse to be the means on one side, ye ought not to be meddlers on the other; but to wait the issue in silence; and unless you can produce divine authority, to prove, that the Almighty who hath created and placed this *new* world, at the greatest distance it could possibly stand, east and west, from every part of the old, doth, nevertheless, disapprove of its being independant of the corrupt and abandoned court of B—n, unless I say, ye can show this, how can ye, on the ground of your principles, justify the exciting and stirring up of the people 'firmly to unite in the *abhorrence* of all such *writings*, and *measures*, as evidence a desire and design to break off the *happy* connexion we have hitherto enjoyed, with the kingdom of Great-Britain, and our just and necessary subordination to the king, and those who are lawfully placed in authority under him.' What a slap in the face is here! the men, who, in the very paragraph before, have quietly and passively resigned up the ordering, altering, and disposal of kings and governments, into the hands of God, are now recalling their principles, and putting in for a share of the business. Is it possible, that the conclusion, which is here justly quoted, can any ways follow from the doctrine laid down? The inconsistency is too glaring not to be seen; the absurdity too great not to be laughed at; and such as could only have been made by those, whose understandings were darkened by the narrow and crabby spirit of a despairing political party; for ye are not to be considered as the whole body of the Quakers but only as a factional and fractional part thereof.

Here ends the examination of your testimony; (which I call upon no man to abhor, as ye have done, but only to read and judge of fairly;) to which I subjoin the following remark; 'That the setting up and putting down of kings,' most certainly mean, the making him a king, who is yet not so, and the making him no king who is already one. And pray what hath this to do in the present case? We neither mean to *set up* nor to *put down*, neither to *make* nor to *unmake*, but to have nothing to *do* with them. Wherefore, your testimony in whatever light it is viewed serves only to dishonour your judgment, and for many other reasons had better have been let alone than published.

First. Because it tends to the decrease and reproach of all religion whatever, and is of the utmost danger to society, to make it a party in political disputes.

Secondly. Because it exhibits a body of men, numbers of whom disavow the publishing political testimonies, as being concerned therein and approvers thereof.

Thirdly. Because it hath a tendency to undo that continental harmony and friendship which yourselves by your late liberal and charitable donations hath lent a hand to establish; and the preservation of which, is of the utmost consequence to us all.

And here without anger or resentment I bid you farewell. Sincerely wishing, that as men and christians, ye may always fully and uninterruptedly enjoy every civil and religious right; and be, in your turn, the means of securing it to others; but that the example which ye have unwisely set, of mingling religion with politics, *may be disavowed and reprabated by every inhabitant of* AMERICA.

FINIS

The

AMERICAN CRISIS I

INTRODUCTION TO

THE AMERICAN CRISIS

Tom Paine's career as a political activist and pamphleteer did not end with the publication of *Common Sense*. In July 1776 he was appointed aide-de-camp to General Nathanael Greene. He began his next writing project, *The American Crisis*, while still in active service in the army, but in April 1777 he accepted the position of secretary to the Committee on Foreign Affairs of Congress. Although the position had a fancy title, it was created with the intention of giving Paine the free time, and a decent stipend, to continue his writings in support of the patriot cause. He would write thirteen essays in the series between December 1776 and December 1783, all aimed at bolstering American morale against what Paine consistently described as a corrupt and loathsome British enemy.

This Penguin Civic Classics volume ends with

the first installment of Paine's American Crisis essays. The months of November and December 1776 were difficult ones for the American army; Paine was part of the retreat from Fort Washington on the east bank of the Hudson River in New York through New Jersey, reaching Trenton on December 4. At that point Paine left Trenton "in order to get out some publications, as the printing presses were then at a stand and the country in a state of despair." His first essay, beginning with the famous words, "These are the times that try men's souls," once again shows Paine at his very best, but this time his task was even more difficult than that which he faced in *Common Sense*: in what he described as a "passion of patriotism," he sought not only to boost American morale, but also to prepare Americans for the long, arduous struggle that lay ahead.

Nearly seven years later that struggle would finally come to an end with the signing of the Treaty of Paris in September 1783. In 1787, Paine returned first to England and then to France, where he would become a passionate defender of the French Revolution in his series of pamphlets, *The Rights of Man*, and later an ardent proponent of deism in his controversial essay *The Age of Reason*. (It was presumably this essay that prompted President Theodore Roosevelt to refer to Paine, unfairly, as "a filthy little atheist.") At this stage in his life, he defined himself not as an Englishman or as an

American, but as a citizen of the world. In 1802, after a tumultuous time in France, including ten months' imprisonment during the reign of Robespierre, he returned to America. There was no hero's welcome waiting for him upon his return—he was now better known as the author of the atheistic *Age of Reason* than as the author of *Common Sense*. His death, on June 8, 1809, went virtually unnoticed. The following day, at his funeral on his farm in New Rochelle, New York, only a handful of friends and neighbors turned out to bid him goodbye. America had, at least for the moment, passed him by. But Paine's American writings, both his bold call for independence and his stirring call for strength and fortitude during the trials of war, have only gained in importance in American memory with the passage of time.

THE AMERICAN CRISIS I

These are the times that try men's souls. The summer soldier and the sunshine patriot will, in this crisis, shrink from the service of their country; but he that stands it *now*, deserves the love and thanks of man and woman. Tyranny, like hell, is not easily conquered; yet we have this consolation with us, that the harder the conflict, the more glorious the triumph. What we obtain too cheap, we esteem too lightly: it is dearness only that gives every thing its value. Heaven knows how to put a proper price upon its goods; and it would be strange indeed if so celestial an article as FREEDOM should not be highly rated. Britain, with an army to enforce her tyranny, has declared that she has a right (*not only to* TAX) but 'TO BIND *us in* ALL CASES WHATSOEVER', and if being *bound in that manner*, is not slavery, then is there not such a thing as slavery upon earth. Even the expression is impious; for so unlimited a power can belong only to God.

Whether the independence of the continent was declared too soon, or delayed too long, I will not now enter into as an argument; my own simple opinion is, that had it been eight months earlier, it would have been much better. We did not make a proper use of last winter, neither could we, while we were in a dependent state. However, the fault, if it were one, was all our own; we have none to blame but ourselves. But no great deal is lost yet. All that Howe has been doing for this month past, is rather a ravage than a conquest, which the spirit of the Jerseys, a year ago, would have quickly repulsed, and which time and a little resolution will soon recover.

I have as little superstition in me as any man living, but my secret opinion has ever been, and still is, that God Almighty will not give up a people to military destruction, or leave them unsupportedly to perish, who have so earnestly and so repeatedly sought to avoid the calamities of war, by every decent method which wisdom could invent. Neither have I so much of the infidel in me, as to suppose that He has relinquished the government of the world, and given us up to the care of devils; and as I do not, I cannot see on what grounds the king of Britain can look up to heaven for help against us: a common murderer, a highwayman, or a house-breaker, has as good a pretence as he.

'Tis surprising to see how rapidly a panic will sometimes run through a country. All nations and ages have been subject to them. Britain has trembled like an ague at the report of a French fleet of flat-bottomed boats; and in the fourteenth [fifteenth] century the whole English army, after ravaging the kingdom of France, was driven back like men petrified with fear; and this brave exploit was performed by a few broken forces collected and headed by a woman, Joan of Arc. Would that heaven might inspire some Jersey maid to spirit up her countrymen, and save her fair fellow sufferers from ravage and ravishment! Yet panics, in some cases, have their uses; they produce as much good as hurt. Their duration is always short; the mind soon grows through them, and acquires a firmer habit than before. But their peculiar advantage is, that they are the touchstones of sincerity and hypocrisy, and bring things and men to light, which might otherwise have lain forever undiscovered. In fact, they have the same effect on secret traitors, which an imaginary apparition would have upon a private murderer. They sift out the hidden thoughts of man, and hold them up in public to the world. Many a disguised Tory has lately shown his head, that shall penitentially solemnize with curses the day on which Howe arrived upon the Delaware.

As I was with the troops at Fort Lee, and marched with them to the edge of Pennsylvania, I am well acquainted with many circumstances,

which those who live at a distance know but little
or nothing of. Our situation there was exceedingly
cramped, the place being a narrow neck of land
between the North River and the Hackensack.
Our force was inconsiderable, being not one-
fourth so great as Howe could bring against us.
We had no army at hand to have relieved the garrison, had we shut ourselves up and stood on our
defence. Our ammunition, light artillery, and the
best part of our stores, had been removed, on the
apprehension that Howe would endeavour to pen-
etrate the Jerseys, in which case Fort Lee could be
of no use to us; for it must occur to every thinking
man, whether in the army or not, that these kind
of field forts are only for temporary purposes, and
last in use no longer than the enemy directs his
force against the particular object which such forts
are raised to defend. Such was our situation and
condition at Fort Lee on the morning of the 20th
of November, when an officer arrived with information that the enemy with 200 boats had landed
about seven miles above; Major General
[Nathanael] Greene, who commanded the garrison, immediately ordered them under arms, and
sent express to General Washington at the town of
Hackensack, distant by the way of the ferry = six
miles. Our first object was to secure the bridge
over the Hackensack, which laid up the river between the enemy and us, about six miles from us,
and three from them. General Washington arrived

in about three-quarters of an hour, and marched at the head of the troops towards the bridge, which place I expected we should have a brush for; however, they did not choose to dispute it with us, and the greatest part of our troops went over the bridge, the rest over the ferry, except some which passed at a mill on a small creek, between the bridge and the ferry, and made their way through some marshy grounds up to the town of Hackensack, and there passed the river. We brought off as much baggage as the wagons could contain, the rest was lost. The simple object was to bring off the garrison, and march them on till they could be strengthened by the Jersey or Pennsylvania militia, so as to be enabled to make a stand. We staid four days at Newark, collected our out-posts with some of the Jersey militia, and marched out twice to meet the enemy, on being informed that they were advancing, though our numbers were greatly inferior to theirs. Howe, in my little opinion, committed a great error in generalship in not throwing a body of forces off from Staten Island through Amboy, by which means he might have seized all our stores at Brunswick, and intercepted our march into Pennsylvania; but if we believe the power of hell to be limited, we must likewise believe that their agents are under some providential control.

I shall not now attempt to give all the particulars of our retreat to the Delaware; suffice it for the present to say, that both officers and men, though greatly harassed and fatigued, frequently without rest, covering, or provision, the inevitable consequences of a long retreat, bore it with a manly and martial spirit. All their wishes centred in one, which was, that the country would turn out and help them to drive the enemy back. Voltaire has remarked that King William never appeared to full advantage but in difficulties and in action; the same remark may be made on General Washington, for the character fits him. There is a natural firmness in some minds which cannot be unlocked by trifles, but which, when unlocked, discovers a cabinet of fortitude; and I reckon it among those kind of public blessings, which we do not immediately see, that God hath blessed him with uninterrupted health, and given him a mind that can even flourish upon care.

I shall conclude this paper with some miscellaneous remarks on the state of our affairs; and shall begin with asking the following question, Why is it that the enemy have left the New England provinces, and made these middle ones the seat of war? The answer is easy: New England is not infested with Tories, and we are. I have been tender in raising the cry against these men, and used numberless arguments to show them their danger, but it will not do to sacrifice a world either to their folly or their baseness. The period is now arrived, in which either they or we must change our sentiments, or one or both must fall. And what is a

Tory? Good God! what is he? I should not be afraid to go with a hundred Whigs against a thousand Tories, were they to attempt to get into arms. Every Tory is a coward; for servile, slavish, self-interested fear is the foundation of Toryism; and a man under such influence, though he may be cruel, never can be brave.

But, before the line of irrecoverable separation be drawn between us, let us reason the matter together: Your conduct is an invitation to the enemy, yet not one in a thousand of you has heart enough to join him. Howe is as much deceived by you as the American cause is injured by you. He expects you will all take up arms, and flock to his standard, with muskets on your shoulders. Your opinions are of no use to him, unless you support him personally, for 'tis soldiers, and not Tories, that he wants.

I once felt all that kind of anger, which a man ought to feel, against the mean principles that are held by the Tories: a noted one, who kept a tavern at Amboy, was standing at his door, with as pretty a child in his hand, about eight or nine years old, as I ever saw, and after speaking his mind as freely as he thought was prudent, finished with this unfatherly expression, *'Well! give me peace in my day.'* Not a man lives on the continent but fully believes that a separation must some time or other finally take place, and a generous parent should have said, *'If there must be trouble, let it be in my day, that my child may have peace'*; and this single reflection, well applied, is sufficient to awaken every man to duty. Not a place upon earth might be so happy as America. Her situation is remote from all the wrangling world, and she has nothing to do but to trade with them. A man can distinguish himself between temper and principle, and I am as confident, as I am that God governs the world, that America will never be happy till she gets clear of foreign dominion. Wars, without ceasing, will break out till that period arrives, and the continent must in the end be conqueror; for though the flame of liberty may sometimes cease to shine, the coal can never expire.

America did not, nor does not want force; but she wanted a proper application of that force. Wisdom is not the purchase of a day, and it is no wonder that we should err at the first setting off. From an excess of tenderness, we were unwilling to raise an army, and trusted our cause to the temporary defence of a well-meaning militia. A summer's experience has now taught us better; yet with those troops, while they were collected, we were able to set bounds to the progress of the enemy, and, thank God! they are again assembling. I always considered militia as the best troops in the world for a sudden exertion, but they will not do for a long campaign. Howe, it is probable, will make an attempt on this city; should he fail on this side the Delaware, he is ruined. If he succeeds, our cause is not ruined. He stakes all on his side against a part on ours; admitting he succeeds, the consequence will be, that armies from both ends of the continent will march to assist their suffering friends in the middle states; for he cannot go everywhere, it is impossible. I consider Howe as the greatest enemy the Tories have; he is bringing a war in their country, which, had it not been for him and partly for themselves, they had been clear of. Should he now be expelled, I wish with all the devotion of a Christian, that the names of Whig and Tory may never more be mentioned; but should the Tories give him encouragement to come, or assistance if he come, I as sincerely wish that our next year's arms may expel them from the continent, and the Congress appropriate their possessions to the relief of those who have suffered in well-doing. A single successful battle next year will settle the whole, America could carry on a two years' war by the confiscation of the property of disaffected persons, and be made happy by their expulsion. Say not that this is revenge, call it rather the soft resentment of a suffering people, who, having no object in view but the *good* of *all*, have staked their *own all* upon a seemingly doubtful event. Yet it is folly to argue against determined hardness; eloquence may strike the ear, and the language of sorrow draw forth the tear of compassion, but nothing can reach the heart that is steeled with prejudice.

Quitting this class of men, I turn with the warm

ardour of a friend to those who have nobly stood, and are yet determined to stand the matter out: I call not upon a few, but upon all: not on *this* state or *that* state, but on *every* state: up and help us; lay your shoulders to the wheel; better have too much force than too little, when so great an object is at stake. Let it be told to the future world, that in the depth of winter, when nothing but hope and virtue could survive, that the city and the country, alarmed at one common danger, came forth to meet and to repulse it. Say not that thousands are gone, turn out your tens of thousands; throw not the burden of the day upon Providence, but *'show your faith by your works'*, that God may bless you. It matters not where you live, or what rank of life you hold, the evil or the blessing will reach you all. The far and the near, the home counties and the back, the rich and the poor, will suffer or rejoice alike. The heart that feels not now is dead; the blood of his children will curse his cowardice, who shrinks back at a time when a little might have saved the whole, and made *them* happy. I love the man that can smile in trouble, that can gather strength from distress, and grow brave by reflection. 'Tis the business of little minds to shrink; but he whose heart is firm, and whose conscience approves his conduct, will pursue his principles unto death. My own line of reasoning is to myself as straight and clear as a ray of light. Not all the treasures of the world, so far as I believe, could have induced me to support an offensive war, for I think it murder; but if a thief breaks into my house, burns and destroys my property, and kills or threatens to kill me, or those that are in it, and to *'bind me in all cases whatsoever'* to his absolute will, am I to suffer it? What signifies it to me, whether he who does it is a king or a common man; my countryman or not my countryman; whether it be done by an individual villain, or an army of them? If we reason to the root of things we shall find no difference; neither can any just cause be assigned why we should punish in the one case and pardon in the other. Let them call me rebel and welcome, I feel no concern from it; but I should suffer the misery of devils, were I to make a whore of my soul by swearing allegiance to one whose character is that of a sottish, stupid, stubborn, worthless, brutish man. I conceive likewise a horrid idea in receiving mercy from a being, who at the last day shall be shrieking to the rocks and mountains to cover him, and fleeing with terror from the orphan, the widow, and the slain of America.

There are cases which cannot be overdone by language, and this is one. There are persons, too, who see not the full extent of the evil which threatens them; they solace themselves with hopes that the enemy, if he succeed, will be merciful. It is the madness of folly, to expect mercy from those who have refused to do justice; and even mercy, where conquest is the object, is only a trick of war; the cunning of the fox is as murderous as the violence of the wolf, and we ought to guard equally against both. Howe's first object is, partly by threats and partly by promises, to terrify or seduce the people to deliver up their arms and receive mercy. The ministry recommended the same plan to Gage, and this is what the Tories call making their peace, 'a peace which passeth all understanding' indeed! A peace which would be the immediate forerunner of a worse ruin than any we have yet thought of. Ye men of Pennsylvania, do reason upon these things! Were the back counties to give up their arms, they would fall an easy prey to the Indians, who are all armed: this perhaps is what some Tories would not be sorry for. Were the home counties to deliver up their arms, they would be exposed to the resentment of the back counties, who would then have it in their power to chastise their defection at pleasure. And were any one state to give up its arms, *that* state must be garrisoned by all Howe's army of Britons and Hessians to preserve it from the anger of the rest. Mutual fear is the principal link in the chain of mutual love, and woe be to that state that breaks the compact. Howe is mercifully inviting you to barbarous destruction, and men must be either rogues or fools that will not see it. I dwell not upon the vapours of imagination; I bring reason to your ears, and, in language as plain as A, B, C, hold up truth to your eyes.

I thank God, that I fear not. I see no real cause

for fear. I know our situation well, and can see the way out of it. While our army was collected, Howe dared not risk a battle; and it is no credit to him that he decamped from the White Plains, and waited a mean opportunity to ravage the defence-less Jerseys; but it is great credit to us, that, with a handful of men, we sustained an orderly retreat for near an hundred miles, brought off our ammunition, all our field pieces, the greatest part of our stores, and had four rivers to pass. None can say that our retreat was precipitate, for we were near three weeks in performing it, that the country might have time to come in. Twice we marched back to meet the enemy, and remained out till dark. The sign of fear was not seen in our camp, and had not some of the cowardly and disaffected inhabitants spread false alarms through the country, the Jerseys had never been ravaged. Once more we are again collected and collecting; our new army at both ends of the continent is recruiting fast, and we shall be able to open the next campaign with sixty thousand men, well armed and clothed. This is our situation, and who will may know it. By perseverance and fortitude we have the prospect of a glorious issue; by cowardice and submission, the sad choice of a variety of evils – a ravaged country – a depopulated city – habitations without safety, and slavery without hope – our homes turned into barracks and bawdy-houses for Hessians, and a future race to provide for, whose fathers we shall doubt of. Look on this picture and weep over it! and if there yet remains one thought-less wretch who believes it not, let him suffer it unlamented.

DECEMBER 23, 1776. COMMON SENSE

Cover art for the Penguin Civic Classics series draws from early American ephemera and was initially inspired by Benjamin Franklin's "Join, or Die" political cartoon, a woodcut print of a divided snake first published in the *Pennsylvania Gazette* in 1754 to stress the importance of colonial unity. Reinterpreted in modern graphic style, these evocative images and symbols have continued to provoke and inspire into the present day.

———◆———

The text is set primarily in Adobe Caslon, a version of which was used extensively throughout America's colonial period. Indeed, the first printings of the Declaration of Independence and the Constitution were printed in Caslon.